TASCAM
30 YEARS OF RECORDING EVOLUTION

by Randy Alberts

HAL•LEONARD®
CORPORATION

7777 W. BLUEMOUND RD. P.O. BOX 13819 MILWAUKEE, WI 53213

ISBN 0-634-01156-1

HAL•LEONARD® CORPORATION

7777 W. BLUEMOUND RD. P.O. BOX 13819 MILWAUKEE, WI 53213

Copyright © 2003 by HAL LEONARD CORPORATION
International Copyright Secured   All Rights Reserved

No part of this publication may be reproduced in any form or by any means without the prior written permission of the Publisher.

Visit Hal Leonard Online at
www.halleonard.com

Contents . TASCAM: 30 Years of Recording Evolution

TASCAM: The Innovations Continue

The modern project studio can trace its lineage through a number of technology breakthroughs. Without a doubt, the introduction of MIDI in 1984, the popularization of modular digital multitrack recorders a decade later (such as TASCAM's DA-88), and the current wave of affordable digital consoles, all mark significant milestones.

Yet thirty years ago, there was no home recording market. In 1969, the first 24-tracks were becoming available, but choices for musicians were few. Some brave souls experimented with consumer "sound-on-sound" decks, layering new elements while recording over original creations; but this "no-undo" process required persistence and luck. At the same time, 4-channel, consumer reel-to-reel decks for the quad market arrived; yet as it had no provision for listening to earlier tracks while adding new tracks, overdubs were impossible.

Among the companies making quad recorders was the TASCAM (TASC AMerica) Corporation, an independent U.S. research, development, and distribution company created in 1971 by TEAC Audio Systems Corporation (TASC) in Tokyo. Dr. Yoshiharu Abe and a small team of techs and marketing pros founded TASCAM in a small office in Marina Del Rey, California. After opening as a custom shop to modify TEAC 4010 quad decks into overdub-capable Simul-Sync TCA-40 Series machines, TASCAM soon began making mixers and recorders for the home recording market. Exhibiting its first products at the Audio Engineering Society (AES) show in 1972, TEAC went on to sell tens of thousands of units to a growing market of musician-recordists—almost single-handedly launching the home recording revolution.

Long before audio education became an industry unto itself, TASCAM gear provided a learn-by-doing sort of self-guided audio apprenticeship. Untold numbers of today's top recording engineers and producers learned the basics of multitrack music production (punch-ins/-outs, console routing, optimizing gain structure, etc.), honing their skills on products such as TASCAM's Model 2, Model 5, and Model 15 mixers. And as small format 4-, 8-, and 16-track recorders emerged, a new industry of garage recording was born, with hundreds of today's large studios starting out from such humble beginnings.

My first TASCAM product was an A-3440 reel-to-reel 4-track that I bought around 1979. I desperately needed to replace a broken-down, way-past-its-prime Dokorder 4-track I'd been using mostly for recording music scores for short independent films and to create voiceovers for early multimedia: film strips, multi-image slide shows, training videos, etc. Compared to the Dokorder, the 3440 was an absolute dream, with a smooth transport and pretty good audio performance—as long as you worked at 15 ips and were careful to optimize signal levels. In fact, that TASCAM deck was good enough to make records on, and my studio partner JJ Jenkins and I would cut a stereo recording of a band live to two of the four tracks, and use the two remaining channels to overdub solos or vocals later. But our real secret was taking the 4-track session tapes (along with our 3440) to local pro studios to mix. We patched that little deck into huge consoles with gobs of outboard gear, and mixed in rooms with quality monitors. We cut a lot of records that way!

Of course, there were other companies that helped shape the home recording boom in the early years, including Otari and Fostex on the multitrack side, and Biamp, Soundcraft, Studiomaster, Tangent, and Tapco on the mixer end. However, it was TASCAM that defined the market. TASCAM-developed formats include the 1/2-inch 8-track, the hugely successful Portastudio 4-track cassette/mixers, the DA-88/38/98/78HR/98HR Hi-8mm MDM's, and the DA-45 24-bit DAT recorder.

TASCAM has been equally successful in supplying solid, dependable tools in other fields of audio production, such as radio/television broadcasting, high-end studio recording, film/video post-production, and the touring/live sound markets. In such endeavors, where reliability is paramount, TASCAM gear is often found next to $500,000 consoles, or in on-air situations where a second take is unheard of.

Today, the innovations continue with products such as the MX-2424 24-track disk recorder and DM-24 digital mixer; but over the years, TASCAM's impact on the way an entire industry makes music has been lasting and significant. Not bad for a company that started off as a small custom shop!

I wonder what TASCAM's up to next.

George Petersen
Editorial Director
Mix magazine

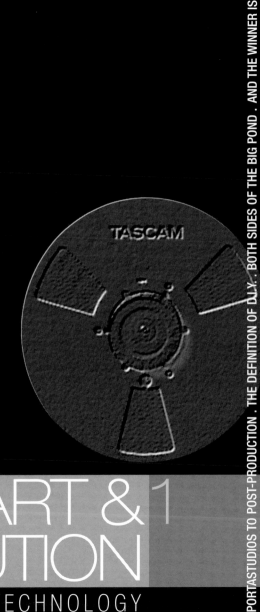

THE ART & 1
EVOLUTION
OF RECORDING TECHNOLOGY

Home Recording Tips

"It puts a little more adventure into recording when you've got to get that vocal before the truck rolls down the hill."

—Greg
HELLO

SLATE IT

Since you can't see what's on the tape, you're going to have to give yourself some kind of a cue so you'll know when to play. It's also a good idea to verbally number each take so it will be easier to find the one you want. If you haven't completely worked out the sequence of the parts you're going to record, you might want to put the count-off and the slate on each track you record on. That way any track can be used as reference when you have to make a choice.

OVERDUB

You don't have to play and sing at the same time. Record each part on a separate track until you get it the way you want it. Then put the tune together with the best examples of each element so that the composite is representative of your best efforts all around.

NOTHING IS FOREVER

different mics at slightly different times, there are situations where the signal they produce together (summed) is less pleasing than the

the relative balance and blend (the mix), then adjust the overall level with the mic input level on the 3340.

TWO MICS, ONE SOUND

You should begin to experiment with stereo mic techniques as soon as possible. Properly done, stereo tracks will often enhance the musical dimensions of the total sound. It's best to use a pair of matched mics—same make and model— but it isn't essential. Watch out for phasing problems. Since the sound will in fact reach the two

and perpendicular to the bridge, the guitar will sound extremely present, larger than life. The bass strings especially will have a lot of punch, it may be too boomy for your taste. In which case you don't necessarily have to move the mic. Try turning down the bass control on your monitoring equipment, and see if you can keep the presence and get rid of the booming. Equalizers, filters and other tone controls are often used to compensate for idiosyncrasies of the sound source you are, the more of the mics. Remember, too, that the further away from you'll be picking up in the mic. Some situations will undoubtedly

Its call to action is as terrifying as it is exhilarating. The opportunity to succeed or fail. And only the unknowing will approach it unprepared. Yet if the truth be known, not all music is

Serious Art

and one of the truly fun and genuinely entertaining musical experiences is playing around with a multitrack tape recorder like the 3340.

REMEMBER IT'S JUST A MACHINE

There's no doubt that the 3340 can do a lot for the music and for the musicianship, but you have to tell it what you want it to do each time you want it to do it. If you expect it to operate itself, you will be disappointed in the extreme. You're going to have to learn which buttons to push and in what sequence. You'll have to learn its proper care and feeding— routine maintenance jobs that are all too easily forgotten. More than this, you'll have to learn how to have patience with yourself when you make mistakes.

HELLO PEOPLE

One has to admire the patience and dedication of the Hello People. Rather than rush into a record company contract or a major concert tour, the Hello People have kept a low profile and refined their music and stage act to the point where now they are ready to showcase their trademark brand of mime-rock. Unlike many bands, they began from the outset with a unique entertainment concept, a blend of music and theater. They sing but they do not speak. Instead they introduce their songs and structure their concert performance with pantomime routines. After years of experience the result is a thoroughly engaging performance of sight and sound. Originally a New York coffeehouse act, the Hello People have played halls from Carnegie to Berry Farm, appeared with Alice Cooper as well as Todd Rundgren, and performed on shows including the Tonight Show and the Mike Douglas Show. The group now lives in the Los Angeles area, and has just finished "HELLO PEOPLE" produced by Lou Adler for Dunhill.

HOME MADE WITH—TEAC

TEAC
HOME MADE
WITH TEAC

STEREO
TCA 18

TECHNOLOGY AND ART

HELLO PEOPLE — THE STORY
... CREEGO IN STEREO

Digital recording console TM-D4000

TASCAM *Digital recording console TM-D4000*

TASCAM

"I was a tape operator at Abbey Road working on *Let It Be* and *Abbey Road*, and an engineer there had his own demo studio in southeast London. In my spare time I was doing multitrack demos at his studio on a TEAC 3340."

– Alan Parsons
  Producer/Engineer/Artist (Beatles, Pink Floyd, Hollies, Paul McCartney, Alan Parsons Project)

Portastudios to Post-Production

The entrance to TEAC's headquarters in Tokyo, Japan.

TASCAM's UK staff in Watford, England

TASCAM's Nemesys team in Austin, TX.

TASCAM France's staff in Antony Cedex, France.

TASCAM's staff at TEAC headquarters in Tokyo, Japan.

TASCAM'S Mexico staff in Mexico City, DF

The R&D staff at TASCAM's Iruma, Japan plant.

With roots in the 1950s and a 2002 product catalog paving the way for the next fifty years, TASCAM's incomparable audio odyssey is a model of excellence in both millenia. Recording engineers, musicians, and producers love to passionately describe their first TASCAM decks and mixers; just ask one, and the initial mantra of its brick-and-mortar parent company, TEAC (Tokyo Electro-Acoustic Company), befits today's global economy as much as it did Japan's decades ago—"TEAC is in the pursuit of information technology."

TASCAM formally joined the TEAC family in that pursuit in 1974. Initially founded as an independent U.S. company in 1971 to distribute and modify TEAC's quad deck recorders, it took TASCAM less than three years to spark an audio revolution that continues to change the

entered the creative vernacular; that word was first coined by Les Paul in his efforts with Ampex to create a "Sel-Sync" recorder that allowed him to record multiple tracks of his intricate guitar parts alongside Mary Ford's lush vocal harmonies on the same tape. TEAC's more affordable "Simul-Sync" recorders soon followed, and recorded music would never sound the same again.

Generating its biggest month in company history in August 2000, TASCAM today continues to build on its leadership role in music and recording technology. Generations of talented TASCAM and TEAC engineers have teamed up over the past three decades to design a gallery of audio "firsts" without parallel. Other companies followed suit with unique innovations, but it's anyone's guess as to how long it would have taken for the

TASCAM's 2002 staff photo at 7733 Telegraph Road in Montebello, California.

way we record and listen to music today. The early phonograph recordings of the twentieth century captured the essence of composition, but were limited to live performance long before "overdub"

world's first 1/2-inch multitrack, 4-track cassette recorder, R-DAT machine, affordable 24-track/24-bit digital recorder, and scratchable CD player to be created—if ever.

It took TASCAM less than three years to spark an audio revolution that continues to change the way we record and listen to music today.

The Definition of D.I.Y.

In-depth interviews for this book with company alumni, and testimonials from respected musicians, engineers, and producers, revealed three denominators common to all—a passion for making music, recording it, and TASCAM. Ask a Grammy-winning artist, novice recordist, or anyone reading this book to recall their first multitrack recording experience, and you'll hear the same story again and again. All degrees of success, age, talent, and musical genre dissipate at the mere mention of names like 80-8, Portastudio, DA-88, or MX-2424.

Any musician inspired by the Beatles, Jimi Hendrix, Quincy Jones, Bruce Springsteen, and countless others has dreamt of what they could create if only they could afford the same tool belt. What was your first multitrack experience like? For many, it involved a struggling young band frustrated with costly studio sessions that rushed the creative process, and rarely captured the group's best musical moments. Whether you were into rock 'n' roll, reggae, or rockabilly, the promise of affordable home recording would eventually change your life.

"My band had an A-2340 4-track when TEAC was just beginning to make home recording a viable option," recalls Gene Joly, TEAC's Vice President of Operations. "Our whole mindset changed with that machine. We were a cover band into Cream and country rock, and Neil Young's *After the Gold Rush* was just huge for us then. But once we got that TEAC, we started recording our own songs and listening to more innovative bands like King Crimson, ELP, Gentle Giant, Genesis, and *Fragile*-era Yes. They inspired us to use our 2340 in our chilly, New England barn to record a Minimoog arrangement of Rimsky-Korsakov's *Night on Bald Mountain*, too."

Numerous recollections like the one above are sprinkled throughout *TASCAM: 25 Years of Recording Evolution*, but brilliantly engineered gear isn't all the company is known for. Be it 1971 or 2001, TASCAM has always led the way in teaching those new to recording how to make the learning curve transparent to the creative process. Many of today's top engineers and producers perfected their skills on 4-channel mixers while reading TASCAM booklets like *The Multitrack Primer*, and just a mention of the *Home Made With TEAC* vinyl album can make a bunch of tough recording musicians downright misty-eyed. The impassioned liner notes in that LP jacket, written by Dick Rosmini and Budd Johnson, created a bond with recordists of all genres that exists to this day at TASCAM:

"The 3340 is part of the continuing search of the artist to control the environment of their creativity with the best tools possible. With it you can get in, around, and behind your music, and in the process gain new insights into the relationships of the parts to the whole. If a musical instrument is an extension of you, the multitrack tape recorder is an expansion and multiplication of yourself. Only time will tell what effect the multitrack recorder will have on the music of tomorrow, but in the meantime, it continues to be a part of the magic that underlies the creative process."

Both Sides of the Big Pond

The tandem of TEAC engineering and TASCAM's expertise and passion for music would not have been possible without the successful bonding of two cultures. Fusing the Japanese work ethic with American rock 'n' roll in the 1970s didn't come without a few snags; but both sides of the TEAC and TASCAM pond

TASCAM than it ever was—a feat many less fortunate, offshore partnerships have failed to harness.

Unlike most Japanese-based companies, much of TASCAM's product design and development in the early years came from the States. Though wary of a new

> "They would banter back and forth about what to do; that's what led to the breakthrough products that came from that company. Know your industry, know your people, and find out how to make their dreams come true."

made a point of getting to know and understand one another. That potent combination of engineering excellence and California vision is stronger today at

marketplace that required vast company resources to develop in the early '70s, TEAC soon came to trust the experience and know-how of the new TASCAM team.

"David Oren was the first person to lay the groundwork for the collaboration between the U.S. and Japan," says Rick Clark, an agency professional who helped produce many of TASCAM's marketing pieces over the years. "They would banter back and forth about what to do; that's what led to the breakthrough products that came from that company. Know your industry, know your people, and find out how to make their dreams come true."

One of many stories that illustrate how well the two cultures co-exist involved a long-time TASCAM employee who needed to shift his life's focus. Stepping down as the company's national sales manager to become a sales rep in order to spend more time with his family, Chuck Prada thought he was in for a rough trip when he was flown to Tokyo to meet with TEAC management.

> "Mr. Norio Tomura was president of TEAC America when I began to work with TASCAM. He was always the quiet, soft-spoken fellow in the back of the room who never took credit for a thing—but he was at the heart of what made that company successful."

"That's traditionally never done in a Japanese company," says Prada. "You either move up or out—never down—and work always comes before religion and family. Mr. Tamura, the president of TEAC Japan, and Mr. Yamaguchi both took me out to dinner, and I thought they would try hard to get me to carry on as their national sales manager. But instead, they understood how much my family meant to me, and we talked about nothing but our three families the entire evening."

"TEAC was one of the first companies that really recognized the benefit of working hand-in-hand with the American market," says Roger Maycock, TASCAM's Marketing Support Manager from 1994 to 1998. "One must understand that a Japanese company has a tremendous amount of pride. TASCAM and TEAC have managed to get past all that—and in the process, have seen it was the right thing to do. They now have a research and development lab, and partnerships with technology companies that would've been unthinkable just five years ago."

Clark agrees. "Mr. Norio Tamura was president of TEAC America when I began to work with TASCAM. He was always the quiet, soft-spoken fellow in the back of the room who never took credit for a thing—but he was at the heart of what made that company successful. He trusted and provided encouragement to the people at TASCAM in a way that allowed them to achieve their personal bests—which is not at all common in companies with overseas headquarters."

TASCAM has become increasingly States-centric over the past decade in terms of engineering and product development. PARC (Palo Alto Research Center), TASCAM's new software development lab, and partnerships with Timeline, Frontier Design Group, Steinberg, Antares, TC Electronic, and others are helping TASCAM to design digital products built for the 21st century. Seven new product specialists have been added to the team, and the manuals for TASCAM's last three major product releases were each written in the U.S.

Mike McRoberts, TASCAM's International Product Development Manager since 1998, is an integral element in this new era of collaboration. His first trip to Tokyo to discuss TASCAM's direction resulted in TEAC asking him to take over its global product development reins, as well as to join them in an evening at the local karaoke bar.

"It's not about simply demanding the products we want," says McRoberts. "It's more about laying out the process of how to develop the product and the steps involved to do so, so we get along great with the folks in Tokyo. I've never in my life been to a karaoke bar in the U.S., but over there it's a way of life: you have a couple of beers and you're up there singing! We have a great time together."

And The Winner Is...

If the number of awards an organization received were the only gauge of its greatness, TASCAM could have rested on its laurels long ago. Acknowledged by magazines and trade groups every year since 1983, the company is more interested in building innovations than

blowing its own trumpet. There is a "mini wall of fame" at the company's Montebello headquarters, but one must walk deep into the corporate offices to find it. Tucked away in a nondescript hallway leading to the TASCAM warehouse, the few plaques displayed there represent but a dusty fraction of the awards the company has received.

Having already received an Emmy from the Academy of Television Arts & Sciences in 1995 for the DA-88, TASCAM

was bestowed with its second Emmy award in five years for Outstanding Achievement in Engineering Development for the MMR-8 and MMP-16 tandem on July 11, 2000. The Academy press release following that second award said it all:

"The MMR-8/MMP-16 and DA-88 are two of the very few such audio offerings to ever win this award. TASCAM is literally the only pro audio equipment manufacturer in the world to have ever won an Emmy twice within such a narrow time frame."

Yet less than one year later, TASCAM was at it again, this time sharing the award with its partner Timeline, as the MMR-8 brought home Oscar gold at the Scientific and Technical Academy Awards in March 2001. Given to but a few developers of "discoveries or inventions of special and outstanding value to the arts and sciences of filmmaking that also have a proven history of use in the motion picture industry," the award is also for the MMR-8's ability to afford its users a more cost-effective means of mixing and playing back digital audio tracks, individually slipping tracks in multiple track configurations, and destructively and nondestructively editing tracks "to eliminate the requirement for razor blade conforming" all together. ◉

If the number of awards an organization received were the only gauge of its greatness, TASCAM could have rested on its laurels long ago.

Master Timeline

FORMATS

- First 35mm magnetic film editor (*Moviola*)
- First 5-channel Todd-AO movie released (*Oklahoma*)
- First magnetic soundtracks
- 4-channel CinemaScope introduced
- dbx introduced
- Dolby Stereo introduced
- *Star Wars* released in Dolby Surround
- First mono Nagra recorder
- First Dolby Surround release (*A Star Is Born*)
- First Dolby movie released (*A Clockwork Orange*)
- Digital 2-track timecode intro
- U-matic format video recorder co-developed with Sony

MILESTONES

- TEAC founded December 24, 1956
- First TASCAM ad in *Rolling Stone*
- First TEAC service centers established in U.S.
- K. Tani invents first Japanese phono disc-cutting system
- TASCAM Corp. acquired by TEAC
- TASC formed in Tokyo
- First Model 10s & Series 70s shipped in U.S.
- K. Tani invents slow-motion video playback for Tokyo Olympics
- TASCAM Corp. founded in Marina Del Rey, CA
- First TASCAM booth at AES/Los Angeles Hilton
- PPG Wave synt
- AES/New York
- Minimoog introduced
- TASCAM moves to TEAC headquarters in Montebello, CA
- First Simul-Sync recorder (A-4010)
- First Simul-Sync cassette (12

- Beatles record *Sgt. Pepper's* on a 4-track

- First 1/2-inch multitrack (Series 70) • First 4-track cassette (144 Portastudio)

EMPLOYEE TENURES

Hajime Yamaguchi ---

Budd Johnson ---|

David Oren --

Rick Clark ----------|

Bill Mohrhoff --

J

PRODUCTS

- TEAC A-4010
- Model 5
- TEAC 124 Syncaset
- TEAC A-4020
- Model 25-2
- 85-16
- TCA-42
- 80-8
- Model 144 Portastudio
- TEAC 2340
- DX-8
- TEAC 3340
- Model 15
- Mod
- Series70
- Model 1
- TEAC 3440
- Model 10
- Model 2
- System 20
- 90-16
- TASCAM 122

| 1956 | 1970 | 1975 | 1980 |

corders introduced
MIDI spec published by MMA
First CD players introduced

- 1/2-inch 16-track introduced
- CD-R introduced
- Digital 24-track introduced
  - Timecode DAT introduced
  - Dolby AC-3 introduced (*Batman*)
- DAW hard disk recorders introduced

- Dolby Digital introduced
  - Sony SDDS introduced (*Last Action Hero*)
  - MD recorders introduced
    - Digital-S film introduced
  - DTS discrete 5.1 introduced (*Jurassic Park*)

- MMR-8 wins TASCAM's second Emmy

- ADAT introduced AES/New York

- DA-88 wins Emmy
- DA-88 introduced AES/San Francisco
- MMR-8 wins Oscar

- MMR-8/MMP-16 win Emmy

- First Hi-8 MDM recorder (DA-88)

2-track, 4-channel cassette (225 Syncaset)
- First 8-track recorder/mixer combo (Studio 8)
First battery-operated multitrack cassette (Porta One)
- First 8-track cassette (238 Syncaset)
- First legal DAT in U.S. (DA-50)

- First 24-bit/24-track recorder (MX-2424)
- First 24-bit R-DAT recorder (DA-45HR)
  - First scratchable/beat-matching CD player (CD-302)

-->
---|
nd tenure --->
---| Mohrhoff 2nd tenure ---------|
regg Hildebrandt --->
--->
Neal Faison --->
Chuck Prada --->
Karl Moet -->
Casey Zygmont --->
Roger Maycock--|
Gene Joly ------------------------------------->
Mike McRoberts ------------------------->

- M-3700
- 644 MIDIStudio
- M-700
- 688 MIDIStudio

- CD-302
- TM-D1000
- DA-45HR
- CD-RW5000

TASCAM 225 Syncaset
- MS-16
- T-Series cassette duplicators
38 & 58
- TASCAM 238 Syncaset

- DA-88

- TASCAM 564
- TM-D8000x
- DA-98HR

- 788 Digital Portastudio
- SX-1 Digital Mixing Environment

CAM 133
- M-2500
- ATR-80/24
- ES-50, ES-60
- DA-800/24 DASH

- DA-P1

- DA-98

- US-428
- CD-R2624

- X-9 DJ Mixer
- GigaStudio & GigaSampler

- TASCAM 388 Studio 8
- Porta One Ministudio
- DA-30
- MSR-24
- DA-50 Pro DAT
- DA-P20

- MD-801R

- MMR-8
- MMP-16
- DA-78HR
- MX-2424

- PCI 822

| 1985 | 1990 | 1995 | 2000 | 2005 |

Awards Chart

PRODUCT	YEAR	AWARD RECEIVED
MMR-8	2000	The Academy of Motion Picture Arts and Sciences (AMPAS)
DA-78HR	2000	TEC Award for *Outstanding Recording Product*
MMR-8/MMP-16	2000	*Outstanding Achievement in Engineering Development Emmy Award* from Academy of Television Arts & Sciences
788 Digital Portastudio	2000	Harmony-Central.com *Hot Pick* at Summer NAMM
MX-2424 & DA-78HR	1999	*PAR Excellence Award* from Pro Audio Review
MX-2424	1999	*Blue Ribbon Best of AES Convention* Award
MMR-8	1999	NAB's 8th Annual *Professionals Choice Award for Best Multitrack Digital Recorder*
DA-45HR	1998	*PAR Excellence Award* from Pro Audio Review
DA-98HR	1998	*Post Magazine's Multitrack Recorder of the Year* Award
DA-98	1998	NAB's 7th Annual *Professionals Choice Award for Best Multitrack Digital Recorder*
DA-88 v. 4.0	1997	NAB's 6th Annual *Professionals Choice Award for Best Multitrack Digital Recorder*
DA-98	1997	*PAR Excellence Award* from Pro Audio Review
DA-302	1997	*PAR Excellence Award* from Pro Audio Review
DA-302	1997	Radio World *Cool Stuff Award* at NAB
DA-88 v. 3.11	1996	NAB's 5th Annual *Professionals Choice Award for Best Multitrack Digital Recorder*
Portastudio 564	1996	*PAR Excellence Award* from Pro Audio Review
Portastudio 564	1996	*Blue Ribbon Best of AES Convention* Award
TM-D8000	1996	*Blue Ribbon Best of AES Convention* Award
DA-88	1996	Readers Choice *Platinum Award*
DA-88	1995	*Outstanding Achievement in Engineering Development Emmy Award* from Academy of Television Arts & Sciences
DA-88	1995	NAB's 4th Annual *Professionals Choice Award for Most Innovative Multitrack Digital Tape Recorder*
DA-P1	1995	Videography *Editors Choice Award* at NAB
DA-P1	1995	NAB *Pick Hit*
DA-P1	1995	Radio World *Cool Stuff Award* at NAB
DA-30 MKII	1995	Music & Sound Awards for *Most Innovative Recording Product*
DA-88	1994	*Mix Magazine* TEC Award for *Best Recording Device/Storage Technology*
DA-88	1994	Music & Sound Awards for *Most Innovative Recording Product*
DA-88	1993	NAB *Pick Hit*
DA-88	1993	Video Platinum Award for *Outstanding Technical Achievement*
424	1992/93	Music & Sound Retailer *Top Ten* Award
488	1992/93	Music & Sound Retailer *Top Ten* Award
M-3500	1992/93	Music & Sound Retailer *Top Ten* Award
424	1992	Music & Sound Awards for *Most Innovative Recording Product*
424	1991/92	Music & Sound Retailer *Top Ten* Award
488	1991/92	Music & Sound Retailer *Top Ten* Award
M-3500	1991/92	Music & Sound Retailer *Top Ten* Award
–	1991	International Special Olympics, Major Sound Donor
M7/MFA faders	1991	EQ *Best In Show Award* at AES
688 MIDIStudio	1990	Music & Sound Awards for *Most Innovative Recording Product*
–	–	Mix Foundation for Excellence In Audio *Silver Sponsor*
–	May 1988	*Home Recording Month Award* from cities of Los Angeles, Chicago, Oakland, Santa Ana, San Diego
–	1987	Broadcast Engineering award for *Advertising Excellence*
"Getchagoin Pack"	1987	Music & Sound Awards for *Most Innovative Manufacturer Promotion* (Porta One, mic, tapes, headphones, how-to booklets)
Studio 8	1986	Music & Sound Awards for *Most Innovative Recording Product*
–	1986	DJ Pro Audio Award for *Leadership, Education & Sales on Recording*
–	1985	Broadcast Engineering Award for *Advertising Excellence*
–	1983	Broadcast Engineering Award for *Advertising Excellence*

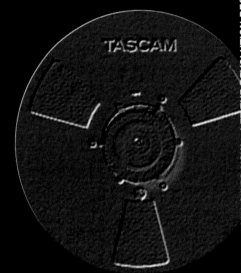

TECHNOLOGY 2
TIMELINE

FROM THE BEGINNING: 1953 – 1969

THE KING OF SOUND TECHNOLOGY . BOTH SIDES NOW . LET THE REVOLUTION BEGIN

Katsuma Tani co-founded TEAC with his brother to build and market one of the first remote recording systems in the world.

Hajime Yamaguchi, President of TEAC Corporation of America.

Norio Tamura, Chairman of the Board, TEAC Corporation.

The King of Sound Technology

TEAC's Iruma manufacturing facility is a brisk 45-minute drive from the main office in Tokyo.

The TEAC museum houses over 3,000 vintage recording systems at the company's headquarters in Tokyo.

An early TEAC 3340 receiving a final check before heading to the U.S.

A glance back at TASCAM's groundbreaking accomplishments over the past 25 years could never begin without retracing TEAC's earliest audio endeavors. In fact, every TASCAM DAT machine, CD burner, digital mixer, cassette Portastudio, and DTRS recorder today owes a debt to the day Tomoma Tani brought home a handmade 3-motor, 3-head stereo tape recorder for his older brother Katsuma to inspect in 1956.

Already known in Japan as the "King of Sound Technology," K. Tani had developed the first phono disc-cutting system made in Japan while working for the Tokyo Television Acoustic Company in the late 1950s—the company that ultimately became today's TEAC. The system was field-modifiable "to record on-site audio programming," and was used extensively by the Japanese Broadcasting Company (NHK) as such. NHK also commissioned K. Tani to invent and build a slow-motion color video playback system that went on to garner global acclaim during the 1964 Olympic Games in Tokyo.

Fascinated by the 3-head recorder before them, and confident they could out-engineer it, K. Tani and his brother T. Tani created the Tokyo Electro-Acoustic Company (TEAC) on December 24th, 1956, to build and sell the new audio system. From that day forward, the slogan "Quality, Cost, Deliver" has adorned production line banners and inspired generations of those who have ever dreamed of, designed, manufactured, sold, marketed, supported, or used a TASCAM product.

TEAC's first quad and 4-channel recorders came ashore to the States during a serious influx of, and infatuation with, Japanese reel-to-reel tape machines. Business was booming in global military base exchanges; but those bringing home the recorders had nowhere to service the machines stateside, so the U.S. government starting requiring offshore audio manufacturers to set up service centers before the lucrative base sales could continue.

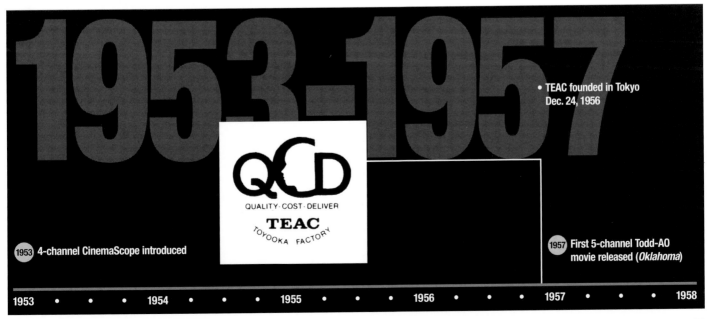

1953-1957

QCD
QUALITY · COST · DELIVER
TEAC
TOYOOKA FACTORY

• TEAC founded in Tokyo
Dec. 24, 1956

1953 4-channel CinemaScope introduced

1957 First 5-channel Todd-AO movie released (*Oklahoma*)

1953 • • • 1954 • • • 1955 • • • 1956 • • • 1957 • • • 1958

One of those service centers was a small brick building in Santa Monica, where TEAC Corporation of America (TCA) was founded. The staff began retrofitting TEAC 2-track and quad tape machines here for what eventually became the first multitrack recording options for the home and professional markets. It didn't take long for early decks like the TEAC A-4010, A-4020, and the TCA-40 series to gain a devoted following of audiophiles and musicians unable to afford expensive studio time or pricier multitracks at the time.

The TEAC A-4010S, originally marketed as a quad recorder deck and sold only through hi-fi audio dealers, was the first Simul-Sync recorder that could overdub new tracks while monitoring previous passes. For the first time, most recording engineers and serious home recordists were able to get into multitrack recording. Its 30 HzN–20 kHz frequency response and 50 dB signal-to-noise ratio were fine in 1966, but limited by today's standards; yet this machine was the spark of every

The A-4020's built-in amplifier and bass speakers teamed with its satellites to reproduce "living sound."

analog and digital multitrack TASCAM would dream up from that point on.

The 4-channel A-4020 soon followed with its built-in amplifier, bass speakers, and two satellite tweeters that are mentioned in the manual as being "spread out for optimum stereo separation and living sound." That same manual has one of the earliest explanations of 4-track recording, often referred to in the mid-1960s as "quarter track" recording .

The TCA-40 Simul-Trak was a 2- and 4-channel stereo playback deck with optional stereo record I/O modules that were "cradled" to create a good-looking modular system. The back panel bristled with an 11-pin record cable that connected to the RA-41 record amplifier, and the machine's unused equalizer, record, and bias sync connector sockets were designated in the manual as "reserved for future 4-channel recording modifications."

"Both Sides Now"

Joining TEAC Japan in 1968 as a sales engineer, Mr. Hajime Yamaguchi is now President of TEAC America and the Managing Director of TEAC Corporation in Japan. His ability to assemble talented teams and step aside as they reinvent recording technology year after year has been a vital part of life at TASCAM. "Our sales strategy is to provide products with storage technology," says Mr. Yamaguchi.

The TCA-42's look was sharp but still reminiscent of the early Simul-Sync deck's home stereo and quadraphonic roots.

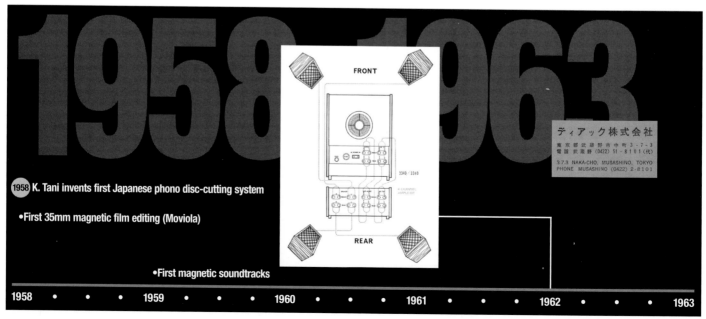

1958 1963

1958 K. Tani invents first Japanese phono disc-cutting system

• First 35mm magnetic film editing (Moviola)

• First magnetic soundtracks

ティアック株式会社
東京都武蔵野市中町 3 - 7 - 3
電話 武蔵野 (0422) 51 - 8 1 0 1 (代)
37.3 NAKA-CHO, MUSASHINO, TOKYO
PHONE MUSASHINO (0422) 2-8101

| 1958 | • | • | • | 1959 | • | • | • | 1960 | • | • | • | 1961 | • | • | • | 1962 | • | • | • | 1963 |

"TEAC has self-developed hardware and firmware, and our growing partnerships have helped strengthen our ability to develop application software and software-based engineering."

Mr. Yamaguchi defers to TASCAM's employees when asked about the future of TASCAM's technology. "Recording technology is definitely changing from tape-based to optical memory devices," he says. "Products are turning more into input devices that will eventually capture data for Internet-based storage systems, so what is really important is the application tool used to achieve this. I have to foresee the future of this company with my eyes and ears wide open in order to make a decision with a positive attitude. I wish I could tell you what's going to happen in the next 25 years, but I always encourage our people to support each other and work together to achieve our common goals."

Let the Revolution Begin

TEAC's early decks provided the spark, but the company's 2340 and 3340 were the first mass-produced Simul-Sync recorders that marked a definitive departure from their quad ancestry. Both had four VU meters on an extensive front panel that included microphone inputs, mic/line level controls, record bias switches, and a selectable tape speed selector to choose between 3-3/4 and 15 ips (inches per second.)

"The 2340 was one of the first 4-track Simul-Sync decks," recalls Jim Lucas, TASCAM's Production Products Group Manager, who managed University Stereo in Sherman Oaks, California, when the new deck was released. "You were either in the music business making records and you said 'Wow, an affordable multitrack system,' or you were in retail and you said, 'Wow, an affordable multitrack system!' The rep brought in a TEAC and I instantly knew I could build a recording studio around it."

Most of the early stateside TEAC manuals in the '60s were predominantly Japanese

with English instructions in the back; but the photos, drawings, and writing style were reminiscent of the accessible Volkswagen manuals of the same vintage era. Like clearly detailing the air vent controls on a '64 Microbus, the early

The legendary 3340 recorded and played back in 2-channel stereo, 4-channel stereo and discrete Simul-Sync, monophonic, and 1/2-track modes.

TEAC manuals were well-written and precisely illustrated to explain basic operation and machine maintenance. This was a trend that would improve with every manual to follow—a daunting task considering the wave of user education

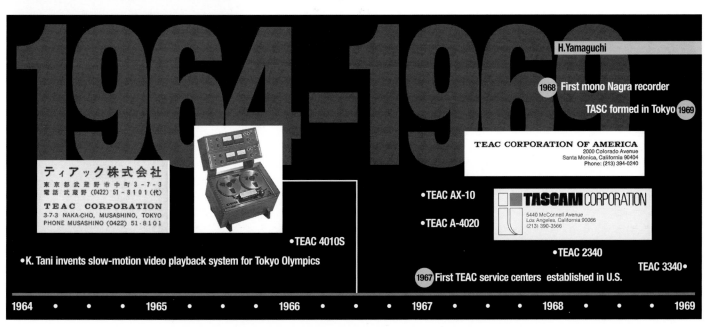

the company was embracing when they first brought multitrack recording products to a market starving for affordable tools.

Explaining 4-track recording to musicians, and showing them how to use the gear efficiently, was no simple undertaking twelve years before the first Portastudio made it a no-brainer. The fact that one could record a complex guitar part, and then concentrate on the vocal performance without performing both live, was news enough then; but learning the concepts and mechanisms of multitrack recording was still a tall order for most. Step-by-step instructions, and the accompanying illustrations and photos went far in the early manuals to help musicians and engineers overcome a new learning and education curve.

The world was dramatically changing in 1969, as was the music reflecting those changes. Early Hendrix, Beatles, and the San Francisco sound, among others, had already opened the audio doors with early multitrack experiments and enough late-night overdubs to change the way we all would listen to and create music forever. That also happened to be the year TASC (TEAC Audio Systems Corporation) Japan was created "to carry out research and development of recording applications for the musicians' marketplace." A timely launch, indeed.

The success of the early Simul-Sync decks, and the demand to educate people on how to use them, made it clear that TEAC needed more than just service centers to fittingly launch its U.S. market. Founded by the Tani brothers in Japan, TASC's "tiger team" in the U.S. was given the lofty goal of building cost-effective, professional audio production gear that performed as good as competitive

products costing three, four, or even six times as much. Eight-track recorders from 3M, Ampex, and others available at the time were going for upwards of $10,000—a lot of money in the early '70s—yet TEAC's special team was able to bring an 8-track recorder to market just a few years later that retailed for a jaw-dropping $4,800.

Heading the U.S. efforts in 1971 was Dr. Yoshiharu Abe, a senior engineer for TEAC Japan at the time. Abe's original core team included Bill Callfield, Andrew Barezza, Budd Johnson, and David Oren. The latter team member, who went on to work for TASCAM for twenty years, remembers a marketplace primed for exactly what TASC was about to unleash.

"Everything that happened here in the U.S. market eventually took place in other countries," recalls Oren. "There were Japanese artists coming over here to work in independent studios to finish albums, who would then take the records back to Japan to get around the lock record companies had on domestic distribution over there. The same thing happened in the U.K., Germany, Scandinavia, and just about everywhere else in the world; but everything started here. There was nowhere else in the world you could do that at the time." ●

> "I've been using TASCAM equipment for a long time now. I had one of the first reel-to-reel 4-track machines they built, and it was a phenomenal machine, man; and I mean great."
>
> – Bo Diddley

TECHNOLOGY TIMELINE 2 CONT.

THE DEFINING DECADE: 1970 — 1979

When You Have More Talent than Money

The Series 70 was the world's first 1/2-inch 8-track recorder.

No decade defined TASCAM products quite like the 1970s did. The dawn of independent music production was taking hold in the U.S. at a time when only contracted artists could afford to multitrack; but the times they were indeed a-changin'. TEAC's solid engineering experience, and TASCAM's intimate knowledge of the U.S. market, allowed both to see a future of affordable recording technology like no other company could. TASCAM's early marketing theme of, "When you have more talent than money," was established as something every musician and engineer could certainly relate to.

Based on TCA's success in the late '60s with the 4010, A-6100, and breakthrough 2340 and 3340 Simul-Sync recorders, Dr. Abe formed the TASCAM (TASC AMerica) Corporation in 1971. Originally modifying TEAC 4010 quad decks for Simul-Sync recording (the TCA-40 Series), TASCAM Corporation was first formed as an independent U.S. distribution company for TASC products. Located at 5440 McConnell Avenue in

Marina Del Rey, California, TASCAM continued to operate as a separate California corporation for three years, developing what would ultimately become the first TASCAM-branded products.

An important date leading to the TEAC and TASCAM partnership was May 10, 1972. Displaying for the first time at the AES (Audio Engineering Society) Show in the Los Angeles Hilton Hotel, TASCAM's booth was where attendees got their first look at the TEAC Series 70 recorders and Model 10 mixer. The quality of the 1/2-inch 8-track recorders came as a big surprise to the standard-bearing, 1-inch 8-track model makers of the day. Based on TEAC's A-7030 transport, the ground-breaking Series 70 was offered in 8-track 1/2-inch, 4-track 1/2- and 1/4-inch, and 2-track 1/4-inch configurations.

The Series 70's spartan front panel sported a cue lever, 4-place tape counter, and basic transport controls, and users could add the Model 701 and Model 501

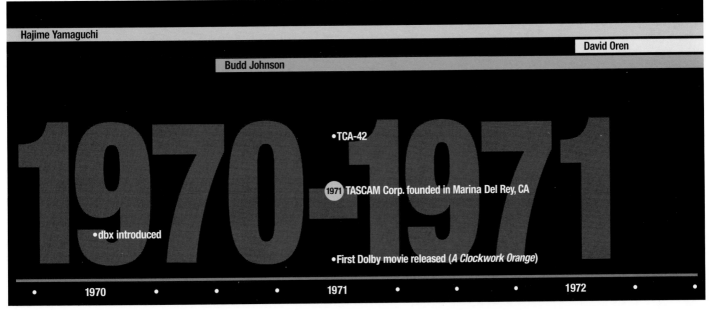

Hajime Yamaguchi

David Oren

Budd Johnson

1970-1971

•TCA-42

1971 TASCAM Corp. founded in Marina Del Rey, CA

•dbx introduced

•First Dolby movie released (*A Clockwork Orange*)

| 1970 | 1971 | 1972 |

record and cue amplifiers to the 70 as well. The simple owner's manual walked new owners through the process of connecting the various components, and included schematics and detailed instructions for properly calibrating and adjusting the recorder. The Series 70 was around for just two years, but it laid the groundwork for the release of the company's legendary 80-8 in 1976.

Released eventually as the first TASCAM-branded product, the TEAC Model 10 mixer was also in the company's first booth at AES in Los Angeles. The mixer included eight input and four submaster modules, and could be upgraded to twenty-four channels with the Model 100 Expander Board. Being the first affordable, professional mixer on the market, the Model 10 was an instant hit at the show; and it also didn't hurt having

Inputs were distributed equally to all four busses and monitors when the Model 107's joysticks were in the center position.

the early support of Westlake Audio and other key dealers when TASCAM needed it most.

"They had a Model 10 in their booth at that AES, too," recalls Budd Johnson, who worked for TASCAM from 1971 to 1976. "Arne Berg taught Westlake's founder, Tom Hidley, about what was going on with the new recorders and mixers—and that did a lot for us in terms of credibility. Westlake was the big pro dealer on the West Coast, so that was a huge help for us in the very beginning."

"I remember the first Model 10 mixer ad," says Gregg Hildebrandt, TASCAM's current Western Sales Manager who worked for West L.A. Music at the time. "That was the first TASCAM ad in the U.S. It just had a picture of the Model 10 and said, '$1,890, plus tax!' It was an 8-input, 4-bus, –10 unbalanced, no-frills

"An Early Evangelist"

David Oren joined TASCAM in 1972 and went on to manage marketing efforts, product planning, and hard disk recording development at various times before leaving the company in 1991 to join Fostex and eventually Panasonic. Oren's leadership in the '70s blazed much of the TASCAM trail in the early days of home recording; a scene not unlike today's emerging DJ market.

"At that point, you were either on a contract with a record company or you didn't go anywhere," Oren recalls. "Our objective was to have artists create their own albums, and that's when the independent record companies came along. You basically had a bunch of indy companies without funding that were telling the artists, 'Give us a demo and we might end up using it.' So that, and the need to be able to get around the major record companies, is really what drove TASCAM and the whole business. You had artists with more time than money on their hands."

Still sounding like the multitrack evangelist he was in 1972, Oren recalls a changing music scene back then. "It was an exciting time in the early '70s because the whole music scene was breaking. The Eagles were just getting hot, and each of them bought 80-8s and mixers to make rehearsal

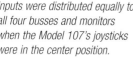

tapes for when they were on the road. We never wanted our products, new or old, to become a barrier between art and creativity. A recorder or mixer couldn't ever fail at just the key moment of someone's music career; it had to work all the time for guys who never cleaned heads, never bought the right accessories, and rarely, if ever, had it properly calibrated."

Before becoming a separate division of TEAC in 1988, TASCAM was initially part of the Hi-Fi Division and was managed by Barry Goldman. Shortly following the TEAC purchase in 1974, TASCAM wasted no time in shipping the first trickle of new products to an anxiously awaiting audio public. The Model 10 mixers began shipping in the summer of that year to U.S. dealers across the country, and the Series 70 recorders followed soon after in the fall.

recording mixer, but it was a very quiet board and considered extremely price-effective compared to anything else at that point in time. It wasn't out of the reach of average musicians back then; for comparison's sake, a black Les Paul Custom was around $999 back then."

Each channel strip in the Model 10 featured 3-band EQ, a 3-position mic attenuation switch, channel assign buttons, and an echo send level control. Users had a number of optional accessories to choose from that included a talkback module, remote control module, and the nifty Model 107 Quad Panner module. The latter strip provided joysticks for continuous panning between the Model 10's four output busses.

"I can still hear that distinctive 'clunk' of the transport when I hit the play button on my first 3340. I thought it was the coolest thing ever invented when I saw the first ad for it and I just had to have one. That first machine taught me how Hendrix and the Beatles made records."

– Joe Chiccarelli
  Grammy-winning
  Producer/Engineer (Beck,
  U2, Tori Amos, Etta James)

The Model 10 mixer eventually became the first TASCAM-branded product.

A New Nameplate

The front lobby entrance is just to the right of the "magnetic recorders" sign in this aerial photograph of the TEAC/TASCAM headquarters in Montebello.

Color-coordinated knobs, five VU meters, and a classy wood case made the TEAC Model 5 a very desirable mixer for a growing number of demo studio owners.

TASCAM's early successes had long since caught the eyes and ears of TEAC Japan. On March 4, 1974, TEAC bought the independent TASCAM Corporation on McConnell Avenue and brought all management, warehousing, and operations under the TEAC umbrella. TASCAM became the official brand name of all TEAC-built recording products designed for the musician and recording markets in the U.S., while TEAC retained exclusive worldwide distribution rights for TASCAM products. That "umbrella" has been at 7733 Telegraph Road in Montebello, California, ever since.

The Montebello headquarters has been home to TASCAM since 1974. Located just twenty minutes from downtown Los Angeles, the company's Telegraph Road address and phone number have not changed in the past thirty years— a rarity given the perpetual change the music and recording industries have gone through since the early 1970s.

One year after introducing the Series 70 and Model 10 at AES/Los Angeles, the company again used AES as a stage for displaying the Model 10 mixer as the first TASC product with a TASCAM nameplate on it. The "TEAC TASCAM Series" debuted at AES in New York's Waldorf Astoria Hotel in September 1973, and the music recording industry would never be the same again. The Model 10's shocking price point made it an instant hit with musicians and recording professionals at all levels.

> "I've used a bunch of TEAC and TASCAM gear over the years. My first 4-track helped me to achieve certain goals that I would not have been able to achieve earlier in my career without TASCAM."
>
> – George Duke
> Producer/Keyboardist/Artist (solo, Herbie Hancock, Cannonball Adderley, Frank Zappa, Clarke/Duke Project, Dianne Reeves)

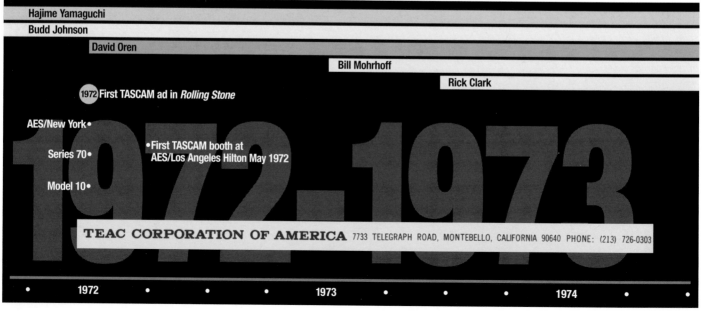

Hajime Yamaguchi
Budd Johnson
David Oren
Bill Mohrhoff
Rick Clark

1972 First TASCAM ad in *Rolling Stone*

AES/New York •

Series 70 •

Model 10 •

• First TASCAM booth at AES/Los Angeles Hilton May 1972

1972-1973

TEAC CORPORATION OF AMERICA 7733 TELEGRAPH ROAD, MONTEBELLO, CALIFORNIA 90640 PHONE: (213) 726-0303

1972	1973	1974

"Selling the Multitrack Dream"

Chuck Prada has come full circle with TASCAM since first becoming a rep for Lienau Associates in 1975, where he sold TASCAM gear for thirteen years. Initially hired by Bill Mohrhoff and Gregg Hildebrandt, he joined TASCAM in 1988 as a regional sales manager to help get the Professional Audio division off the ground. Prada went on to become Field Sales Manager and National Sales Manager before returning again to his favorite pastime—reping TASCAM products.

"As a rep, you sometimes have to sell lines you don't completely believe in," Prada says. "But I believed in everything that TASCAM did, then and now. If I were to summarize everything, I would say that everyone should have the opportunity to work for a Japanese company like TEAC, and I mean that sincerely. I commented after my first trip to Japan that if my time were about to be up that I could say my life was complete after seeing the way things are done at TEAC in Tokyo. The teamwork, the vibration, and the feeling was great; and everybody went way out of their way to make me feel at home there."

TASCAM's Model 5 mixer debuted the following year in September 1975. Following in the Model 10's modular design footsteps and built with medium-sized 4- and 8-track studio owners in mind, the Model 5B was an 8-input/4-output compact mixer that offered features found on more expensive consoles. Multiple accessory patch points, channel expandability, and a built-in talkback mic were standard equipment, and the mixer's modular construction allowed users to swap mixer components when a module was in need of service or repair. Considerably quieter and more affordable than the Model 10, the 5's user-friendly manual was well-written and included references to the *Home Made With TEAC* instructional album to further help new recordists along.

This picture of a Model 5 mixer without its front panel illustrates a modular design inherited from the Model 10.

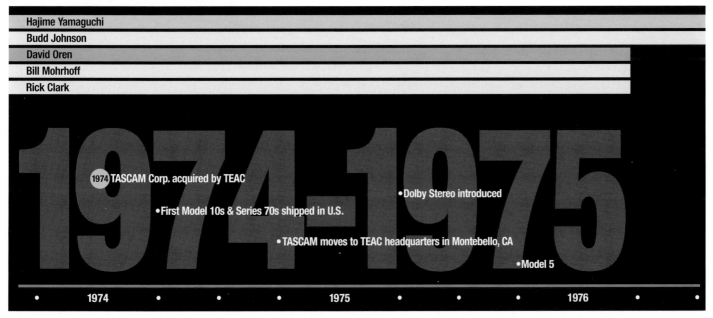

Hajime Yamaguchi
Budd Johnson
David Oren
Bill Mohrhoff
Rick Clark

1974-1975

1974 TASCAM Corp. acquired by TEAC
• Dolby Stereo introduced
• First Model 10s & Series 70s shipped in U.S.
• TASCAM moves to TEAC headquarters in Montebello, CA
• Model 5

1974   1975   1976

An early artist's rendering of TEAC'S Montebello, California headquarters.

Roll Your Own at Home

Sold in the new TASCAM Studio Series line, perhaps no single multitrack recorder was more responsible for the explosion of musical creativity in the early 1970s than the TASCAM 80-8. Though its nameplate still read "TEAC," the 80-8 was TASCAM's biggest product hit—and one that truly began to establish the company as a powerhouse. A staple for many professional recording and post facilities at the time, the 80-8 soon also became popular with artists looking to gain more creative control over their music—to "Roll your own at home," as an early grass roots promotional campaign declared. Numerous supergroups at the time—including the Eagles, Boston, and Kansas—recorded tracks at home, transferring many of those tracks onto commercial studio recorders and ultimately onto countless classic albums. Trying to recreate a demo's spark at $100 an hour in a studio was unlikely, so the 80-8 quickly became popular with artists for capturing the musical spirit of the moment—at home and while on the road.

The 1/2 inch, 8-track 80-8 operated at 15 ips and featured full IC logic circuitry for the transport controls. Output-select buttons controlled the machine's three heads, and a row of function-select switches controlled each of the eight tracks' playback/record statuses. The RC-170 remote control unit was unique in those days, and users could add the optional DX-8 dbx encode/decode processor modules for up to 30 dB of noise reduction—a must in the early days of analog tape for any high-quality recordist.

Following the introduction of the Model 1— the company's first 8 x 2 line level mixer—TASCAM began to improve the audio bottom line with the rackmountable DX-8. Providing eight channels of quiet dbx noise reduction, the DX-8 combined with the 80-8 to provide professional results at a fraction of the cost associated with other pro-level machines.

TASCAM next introduced its 25-2 mastering recorder—a superior reel-to-

"I did a lot of the demos for Utopia in my home studio on a TASCAM 80-8. We each recorded our material in modules at home, and then brought it all back into the studio in various states of completion. I wrote 'Gangrene,' 'Crazy Lady Blue,' and the intro of the *Road to Utopia* album on my 80-8."

– Willie Wilcox

    Drummer/Producer/Sound Designer (Utopia, Todd Rundgren, Hall & Oates, Meat Loaf, Natalie Cole, Luther Vandross, Sci-Fi Channel, USA Networks)

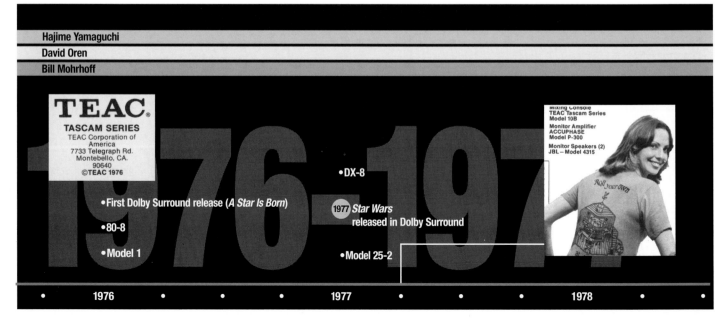

Hajime Yamaguchi
David Oren
Bill Mohrhoff

TEAC.
TASCAM SERIES
TEAC Corporation of America
7733 Telegraph Rd.
Montebello, CA.
90640
©TEAC 1976

•DX-8

Mixing Console
TEAC Tascam Series
Model 10B
Monitor Amplifier
ACCUPHASE
Model P-300
Monitor Speakers (2)
JBL – Model 4315

•First Dolby Surround release (*A Star Is Born*)

1977 *Star Wars* released in Dolby Surround

•80-8

•Model 1

•Model 25-2

1976   1977   1978

The $3,500 TEAC 80-8 TASCAM Series recorder was ruggedly built and comparable to a $10,000 Ampex 8-track machine on the market at the time.

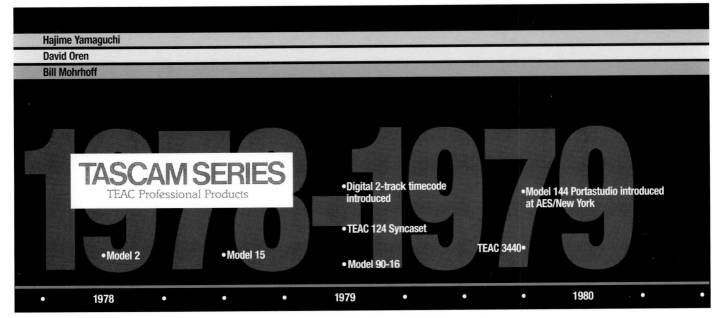

Hajime Yamaguchi

David Oren

Bill Mohrhoff

TASCAM SERIES
TEAC Professional Products

1978-1979

•Digital 2-track timecode introduced

•TEAC 124 Syncaset

•Model 2   •Model 15   •Model 90-16

•Model 144 Portastudio introduced at AES/New York

TEAC 3440•

1978   1979   1980

reel replacement for its predecessor, the 2-track version of the Series 70 recorder. Combined with the 80-8 and DX-8 dbx unit, the 25-2 completed the company's first fully professional record, edit, and mastering studio solution. One year later saw the release of the Model 15 mixer, TASCAM's most professional mixer to date. Though priced at $7,500 and weighing a whopping 400 pounds, the Model 15 was still considerably more affordable than equally outfitted consoles from TASCAM's competitors of the day.

The Model 15 incorporated discrete FET microphone preamps to lower noise and distortion, and RCA connectors were used over costly canon-type connectors to keep the unit's cost so low. Though ballyhooed by the competition as being "semi-pro" for using unbalanced connectors, TASCAM's well-grounded mixer and the DX-8 introduction more than overcame that moniker, as users caught on to the company's professional recording results.

TASCAM's first 1-inch 16-track recorder was released the following year, and included sixteen channels of built-in dbx noise reduction. The first recorder to fit sixteen tracks on 1-inch tape, the 90-16 teamed up with the Model 15 mixer to launch countless studios in those days. Each track of the 90-16 had a single button that switched between tape/source, playback/record, and dbx decode/encode functions simultaneously.

"Jonathan Cain and I wrote 'Can't Take That Away' together one day. I woke up early the next morning and went down to the music room in a robe, and recorded a guitar solo for it before breakfast on my TASCAM 80-8. I just wanted a guide track in place for when he came back to finish the demo that day, but he said, 'It sounds great; why would you want to record it again?'"

– Peter Frampton
Guitarist/Songwriter
(solo, Humble Pie, David Bowie, *Almost Famous* soundtrack)

The Model 15 marked TASCAM's first big step into the high-end professional studio market. Its distinctive padded armrest was comfortable and cool for long sessions.

The 20-Pound Recording Revolution

"Demos in those days were truly

demos; not the master-quality work

you can do at home today. But

people would listen to my demos and

say, 'Wow, this sounds great. You

have a studio?' I'd tell them, 'Yes,

it's a Portastudio.'"

– Simon Phillips

Artist/Drummer/Producer (solo, Jeff

Beck, The Who, Mick Jagger, Stanley

Clarke, Jack Bruce, Toto)

Having defined affordable recording throughout the '70s with a string of product hits, TASCAM's most legendary product line was yet to hatch. The company's ground-breaking work with multitrack cassette recorders was first set forth with the release of the TEAC 124 Syncaset in 1979, and carries on with digital Portastudios to this day. Marketed by TASCAM, the 124 used a Simul-Sync record/playback head to give many musicians their first "multitracking" experience, using cassette head technology sourced in TEAC's sound-on-sound days. Though not a pro unit, the 124 certainly laid the groundwork for what TASCAM was about to unleash on the world.

The AES Show in New York's Waldorf Astoria was once again TASCAM's stage on September 22, 1979, when the company introduced the TEAC 144 Portastudio—the world's first 4-track cassette recorder. Initially dubbed the Model 144, the Portastudio was an instant hit with musicians and hailed by magazines as a revolutionary audio product. Musicians could finally record, overdub, EQ, bounce, and mix down multiple tracks all from the foot of their beds, if need be; and engineers marveled at the 144's ability to squeeze four tracks out of an 1/8-inch cassette tape.

Like so many classic "cocktail napkin" stories, the original plans for the 144 were drawn up on the back of a placemat. In fact, David Oren recalls a Culver City restaurant that inspired more than a few TASCAM and TEAC engineers' design sessions.

"All the original concepts of the Portastudio were sketched out on a Sambo's placemat one night," Oren laughs. "In fact, the PMS 264 color in TASCAM's logo back then was that same classic Sambo's orange! Head technology had to get to the point where we could do something like a 144, and advances in TEAC's core materials and shielding were making that possible at the time. We were able to get frequency responses around 40–28 kHz, which was a lot better than the 60–20 k we were getting with the 80-8 recorder. We were able to do that and get the crosstalk almost nonexistent, and that's when we knew we could move forward and create the Portastudio. Unlike consumer tape heads, the Portastudio heads had four equally spaced tracks and used the same techniques we were perfecting at the time with the 80-8."

"The idea of doing it yourself without going into a recording studio was a far-out concept back then," says Casey Zygmont, a longtime rep selling TASCAM gear since the early 1980s. "That's why the 144 and the 124 were such revolutionary products. They were the first affordable multitracks that you could really do something with without going broke. The Portastudios are what really got TASCAM going."

The Portastudio wasn't met without a few skeptics at first. TASCAM had set up a 144 in a room at the Waldorf during AES to give dealers, reps, and the press a closer look. One rep was playing an acoustic guitar, while another recorded him with an expensive Neumann mic. Apparently, that wasn't a level-enough playing field for some critics.

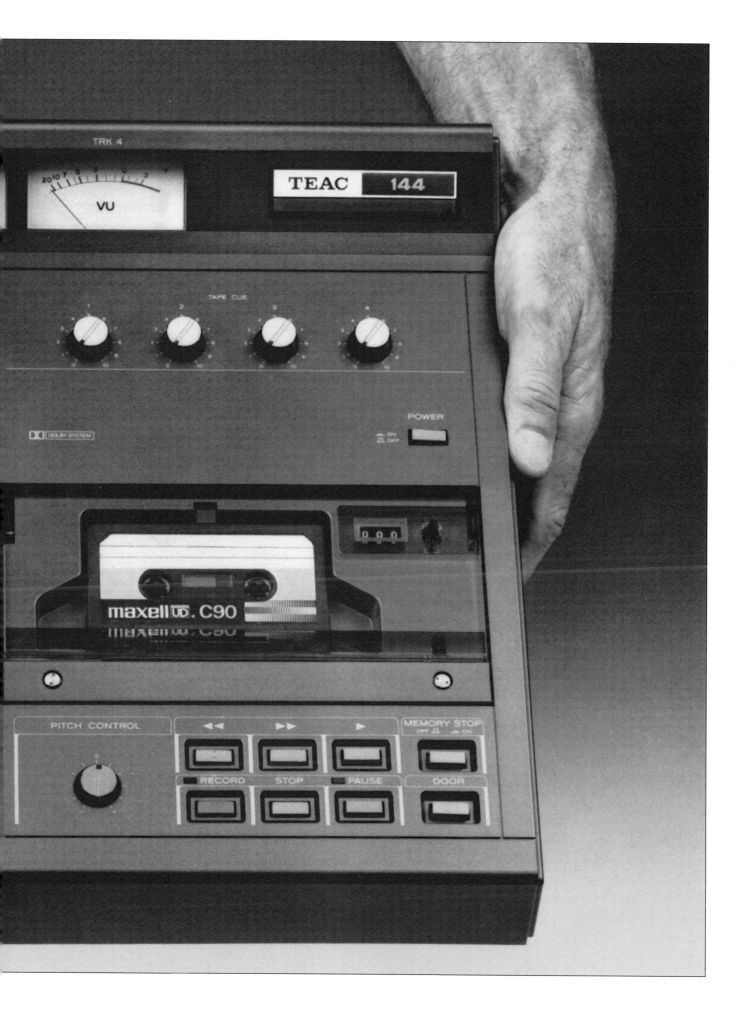

"The 144 had a retail price of $899, and we had a $1,200 Neumann mic plugged into it," recalls Chuck Prada. "The biggest response we got from that was, 'That's not fair!' The whole AES show we were trying to tell people that 'garbage in is garbage out,' but they didn't quite get it at first."

The Portastudio was an all-in-wonder recording solution that sported many features found on the professional recorders and mixers of the day. Each channel in the 4 x 2 mixer had its own fader and pan, bass, treble, trim, aux send, and mic/line controls; also, tracks could be "ping-ponged," and users could overdub and punch record parts for days. The 20-pound Model 144 was a heavyweight when compared to the analog Portastudios of today, but the ability to carry it to gigs and do remote recording with a couple of mics was a blessing to anyone in the late 1970s. ◉

"The 144 was the hippest thing at that time, and later I bought a 244. Both drove me towards becoming a songwriter and getting into engineering. I made all kinds of music with those two machines."

– Jim Keltner
Drummer/Songwriter/Engineer
(Bob Dylan, John Lennon, George Harrison, Neil Young, Ry Cooder, member of the Traveling Wilburys

LEE, SMITH & JAGER
ATTORNEYS AND COUNSELORS
150 SOUTH WACKER DRIVE · SUITE 950
CHICAGO, ILLINOIS 60606
(312) 726-1982

WM. MARSHALL LEE, P.C.
THOMAS E. SMITH
MELVIN F. JAGER
LLOYD L. ZICKERT
WILLIAM M. LEE, JR.
HOWARD H. DARBO
GLENN W. OHLSON
ROGER N. CHAUZA

MARKETING
DEC 1 1983
RECEIVED

TELEX: 724389 TELESPAN
SKO LSJ
TELECOPIER 726-1984
CABLE ADDRESS 'LEESMITH'

November 28, 1983

Mr. David Owens
TEAC Corporation of America
7733 Telegraph Road
Montebello, California 90649

RE: **Mini-Studio** Trademark
File No. 220-1006

Dear Dave:

Enclosed you will find a copy of the trademark search report on your proposed use of **Mini-Studio** for portable multitape recorders and mixers.

You will note from the search results that the trademark **Mini-Studio** had been registered as number 1,004,437 by L.P.B., Inc., of Frazer, Pa. The product involved was studio mixing consoles and turntable units. If this registration was in force, it would bar you from adopting **Mini-Studio** as a trademark for your similar products. However, it was canceled under Section 8 of the Trademark Laws on July 7, 1981. This cancellation resulted from the failure of L.P.B. to file an affidavit of continued use within six years from the date of initial registration. Accordingly, registration no. 1,004,447 is not a bar to your adoption of the same canceled trademark.

The remaining search results show a plurality of uses of the prefix **Mini** and the suffix **Studio** on the same or similar products. For example, **Mini-Tape** is a registered trademark for sound recording apparatus; **Mini-Cassette** is a registered trademark for cassette tapes; **Mini-Store** is a registered trademark for video disk recorders; **Mini-Mix** is a common law trademark for an audio mixer owner by Switchcraft of Chicago; and **Mini-Studio** is a trade name used by a company in Columbus, Nebraska. The search also uncovered your prior registration for **Porta-Studio** for sound mixing apparatus.

In our opinion, the search results failed to uncover any prior trademark which would inhibit your adoption of **Mini-Studio** for portable multitape recorders and mixers. One you adopt this trademark for your proposed product line, it can be registered after it is used in interstate commerce as part of a bonafide commercial sale or shipment. If

Mr. David Owens
November 28, 1983
Page 2

you desire us to register the trademark after its first use, please provide us with the date of first use in interstate and intrastate commerce, and with six samples of the trademark as actually used in interstate commerce.

Please call if you have any further questions.

Very truly yours,

Melvin F. Jager

MFJ:ms
Enclosure

cc Richard B. Silverman, Esq.

Though misspelling his name, this "Mini-Studio" trademark search results letter to David Oren held nothing but good news for TASCAM.

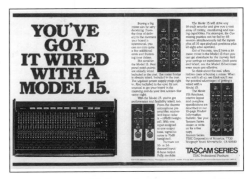

YOU'VE GOT IT WIRED WITH A MODEL 15.

TASCAM SERIES
TEAC Professional Products

Mike McRoberts holding the first Portastudio he sold in 1979 at Solid Sound in Boulder, Colorado—twenty years before becoming TASCAM's International Product Development Manager.

TECHNOLOGY TIMELINE 2 CONT.

MIDI, MACS, AND MORE: 1980 – 1989

SETTING THE STAGE . CARRYING ON THE TASCAM TRADITION . REINFORCING A WORKHORSE
MORE AUDIO INNOVATIONS . HOW DID THEY DO THAT? . THE FIRST LEGAL DAT

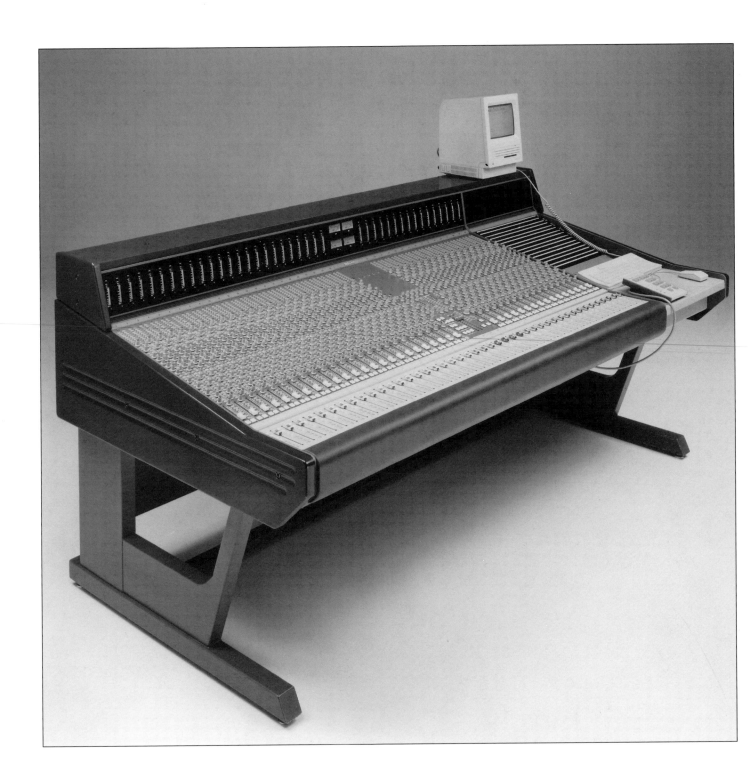

Setting the Stage

The TASCAM 122 was the company's first pro-quality 2-track cassette recorder.

Many of today's top engineers and producers learned their chops on the modular System 20.

The introduction of the legendary TEAC 144 Portastudio in 1979 set the stage for years of achievements to follow. TASCAM's designers were already planning another decade's worth of ground-breaking machines to come by the time the 144 shipped the following year: the world's first 8-track cassette recorder, 8-track reel-to-reel/mixer combo, and rotary head DAT recorder were realized by the time the Berlin Wall came down in 1989.

The 1980s also witnessed the introduction of MIDI (Musical Instrument Digital Interface), a machine "language" that ushered in a new era of creative possibilites and studio connectivity. MIDI ultimately made the desktop computer an indespensible studio tool for professional and home studios at a time when available analog tape tracks were a scarce commodity. By synchronizing their MIDI-savvy gear with multitrack recorders, musicians and engineers no longer had to eat up precious tape tracks with drum machines and synthesizers,

and hardware- and computer-based sequencers quickly became a creative alternative to recording, editing, and mixing music.

Having already established the home recording market in the 1970s, TASCAM was now setting its sights on further developing the company's professional studio product lines. David Oren led the design team's efforts in creating a pro-level, 2-track cassette recorder for the professional market—the TASCAM 122 Studio Cassette Recorder. The rackmounted 122 was the company's first 3-head, 2-speed cassette deck that recorded at 1-7/8 and 3-3/4 ips. The rugged 122 was built like a tank, and featured bias and EQ switches, built-in Dolby noise reduction plus HX expansion, and separately housed record and repro heads that eliminated azimuth error and permitted simultaneous off-tape monitoring. NBC adopted the TASCAM 122 network-wide less than a year after its release; and CBS and ABC soon followed suit to make it an industry standard.

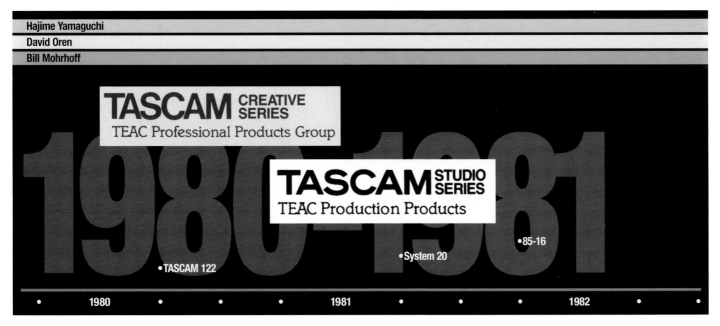

Hajime Yamaguchi
David Oren
Bill Mohrhoff

TASCAM CREATIVE SERIES
TEAC Professional Products Group

TASCAM STUDIO SERIES
TEAC Production Products

1980 1981

•85-16
•System 20
•TASCAM 122

1980   1981   1982

Following up on TASCAM's modular mixer design concepts put forth in the previous decade, the company released the TEAC/TASCAM System 20 in 1981. Targeted at pro studios and Portastudio owners looking to upgrade their home-recording rig, the System 20 included the 6-input/4-output MM-20 mixer, a 4-VU meter bridge, a 4-channel input expander module, a 4-channel parameteric equalizer, and the 22-4 and 22-2 recorders. The expandable System 20 became the heart of many new studios; but having to repatch and reconfigure the system when shifting from multitracking to mixdown proved too complicated for some home studio owners—especially those

accustomed to the simplicity of the Portastudio.

TASCAM's 85-16 multitrack recorder was a big improvement over its 1978 predecessor, the 90-16. The 85-16, which cost 25% less than its older brother, offered an advanced sync head design that allowed users to ping-pong tracks at its full 40 Hz–18 kHz frequency response —the first machine able to do so. The recorder featured special logic circuitry and was packaged with a separate 16-channel dbx noise reduction system that greatly enhanced audio results. Despite a cosmetic miscommunication between marketing and R&D that resulted in

"Carrying on the TASCAM Tradition"

Before Gregg Hildebrandt was hired as TASCAM's Western Regional Sales Manager on July 1, 1984, he worked for Don Griffin at West L.A. Music and the Solomon Company—an independent rep firm in southern California. Living just three blocks from the TASC offices in Santa Monica, Hildebrandt worked hard at getting the company to open up West L.A. Music as a dealer at a time when musicians were hungry for what TASCAM was building.

"For months, I spent virtually every morning bringing coffee and donuts to everybody at TASC," Hildebrandt recalls. "We actually were opened up by accident. The TASC Sales Manager was on a trip, and his second-in-command, who

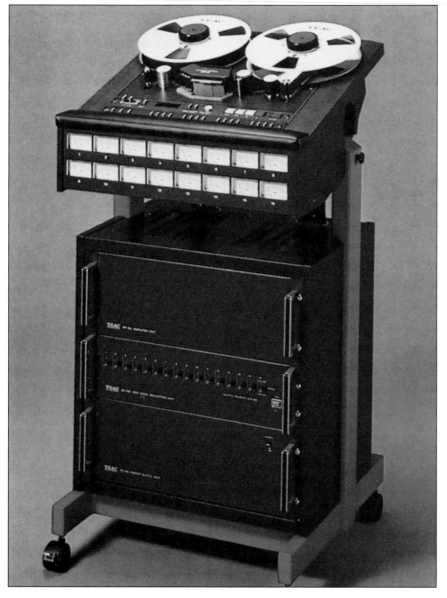

The 85-16's modular dbx processors and bias, record, and playback amplifiers were easily accessed with the front panel removed.

was a West L.A. customer, opened us up; and we quickly became the largest TASCAM dealer in the country. My background was in electronic engineering, so selling TASCAM was my favorite thing at West L.A. Music."

"Our products have always been over-engineered, if anything," Hildebrandt continues. "We rarely had quality issues with our products. We'd try to build a $99 box, but it might have $300 worth of parts at first, because the R&D teams are just so used to building things that are completely bulletproof. The Porta One was phenomenally popular when it came out, but it was a $1,000 piece of gear. Fostex was selling the X-15 for about half as much, so we immediately went to work on its baby brother."

Continued next page

The 85-16, which cost 25% less than its older brother, offered an advanced sync head design that allowed users to ping-pong tracks at its full 40 Hz–18 kHz frequency response—the first machine able to do so.

bright orange support legs, the 85-16 "Flamingo" went on to become a staple recorder for professional music and post-production studios.

Teamed up with the 85-16, TASCAM's Model 15 console mixer began to further establish the company's name with professional 16-track recording studios. The Model 16's stereo solo-in-place and special remix mode features were found only on the world's most expensive boards at the time; and 4-band sweep parametric EQ, discrete Hi-Z FET mic preamps, balanced transformer-isolated XLR connectors, and a built-in audio patchbay rounded out the 16's impressive features. Designed to handle 8- and 16-track recorders, the 16 could also be configured to work efficiently with 24-track recorders.

A real beauty to behold, TASCAM's Model 16 was the company's second large-format console mixer.

Hajime Yamaguchi
David Oren
Bill Mohrhoff

Rick Clark-2nd Tenure

•CD-ROM recorders introduced

TASCAM
TEAC Production Products

1982-1983

•Model 16

• TASCAM 234 Syncaset
•TASCAM 38 & 58
•TASCAM 133

1982   1983   1984

Reinforcing a Workhorse

By 1982, the 80-8 recorder was showing signs of fatigue. Positioning the 80-8 both as a professional studio solution and a recorder for users buying their first 8-track, TASCAM set forth to develop a new machine to take its place: the TASCAM 38.

Shown here atop the 122 mkII master recorder and M-312B mixer, the 1/2-inch 8-track TASCAM 38 was a great replacement for an aging 80-8.

"The 38 was legendary," says Casey Zygmont. "We sold a ton of those. The TASCAM 58 was also supposed to be a top-of-the-line pro machine that we were trying to sell to production, post-production, and commercial studios, but the very first version came over with unbalanced inputs and outputs, so we had to send it back to Tokyo to add balanced I/O. We really struggled in the early '80s trying to find a way into the professional production marketplace."

TASCAM was still being pigeonholed as a "semi-pro" company by the competition in 1983, but the 38 went a long way in squelching that misperception, and became the company's best-selling machine at the time. Fostex's first 1/2-inch 16-track recorder was making headway in the pro market, but some early crosstalk problems prevented it from becoming a serious high-end

"Carrying on the TASCAM Tradition," *continued*

Looking forward to the future direction of the musician and professional markets, TASCAM took notice of the growing number of computers appearing in control room booths. "One of the things Dave Oren felt strong about was that the real market for multitrack products was going to be split between musicians and production people doing video," concludes Hildebrandt. "So we made the first generation of products designed specifically to be synchronized to or controlled by external computers. That started with the 50 Series and then became the 40 series, and when we got into digital, we began working with all the synchronizer manufacturers. That's what put us way ahead in the minds of the high-end professional users."

Hajime Yamaguchi
David Oren
Bill Mohrhoff
Rick Clark-2nd Tenure

Jim Lucas

1984-1985

- First CD players introduced
- MIDI spec published by MMA
- TASCAM 225 Syncaset
- TASCAM 388 Studio 8
- M-2500
- TASCAM 234 Syncaset
- Porta One Ministudio

1984   1985   1986

TASCAM's 133 AV Sync recorder dominated the multi-image production and presentation markets.

> "I remember the first time in 1984
> I ever did a multitrack recording
> on a TASCAM 1/4-inch 4-track. It
> was an easy machine to learn, and
> that just made me want to learn
> more; an amazing machine that
> made my bass sound really huge.
> That recorder made me think I
> was a rock star!"
>
> – Robert Sledge
>
> Bassist/Songwriter
>
> (Ben Folds Five)

machine. It cost $5,000, so many users opted instead to buy two TASCAM 38s.

"My first real recorders were the TASCAM 38 and the Model 32, the accompanying 2-track mixdown deck," recalls Roger Maycock. "The dbx noise reduction module allowed me to do an incredible amount of quality work with those machines. I really credit my 38 and 32 for not only promoting my music career, but for also helping me migrate from being a school music teacher to a whole new career in the music products industry; one that I'm still in. For that reason, TASCAM has a very fond place in my heart."

TASCAM next focused on the multi-image presentation market with its 133 AV Sync Cassette Recorder. The 3-track 133's high-quality stereo heads coupled with a third cue track made it an instant hit for those producing sales presentations, lectures, and trade show displays that incorporated still and video images. Users could layer a 25 Hz Auto Present tone on the cue track that

instructed the 133 to pause and/or rewind to zero at just the right spots during single or continuous presentations. Equally convenient was the unit's ability to interface with analog or digital programmers and mixers, or to drive powered speakers without a mixer or amplifier directly from the 133.

The 133 AV was soon followed by the TASCAM 225 Syncaset, the world's first 2-track, 4-channel cassette recorder capable of recording independently on either track. For just $395, users could do plenty without a mixer or second mixdown cassette deck. The 225 accepted mic and line level inputs, could create mono mixdowns for multi-image and video presentations, and its input mix switch allowed up to two external inputs to be mixed with an existing tape track without ever touching a mixer. The 225 was joined by the TASCAM 234 Syncaset the next year as the first rackmountable 4-track cassette recorder/reproducer with dbx and a 3-3/4 ips tape speed.

43

More Audio Innovations

One look at the shoulder strap said it all for the Porta One Ministudio. The Porta One was more compact and lighter than the Model 144 and 244 Portastudios, and offered dbx noise reduction, four mic/line input jacks, and a VU light defeat switch for extending battery life. West L.A. Music was all over the Porta Ones, though a printer's error in their favor certainly gave them an unexpected head start.

"I got a call late one night from Bill Mohrhoff at TASCAM," Gregg Hildebrandt recalls, "and he told me he'd just shipped us twelve 'Porta Ones'. We didn't even know what it was because they hadn't announced it yet, but Bill told me I'd find out when I opened the store on Sunday. Well, that turned out to be quite a big break for us because the *Los Angeles*

Times had the Porta One on its 'Calendar' section cover that weekend. They were supposed to list all the southern California TASCAM dealers in the story, but accidentally left everyone out but us!"

Another first in 1985 was the TASCAM 388, the only machine of its kind to integrate an 8-track, 1/4-inch reel-to-reel recorder with a professional mixer. Dubbed the "Studio 8", this good-looking, compact package sported eight channels of dbx, was SMPTE/EBU/computer-savvy, and cost less than $4,000.

"That was a very interesting product because it took a lot of what we learned from the the 144 and 244 Portastudios," says Jim Lucas, who started with TASCAM just after the 388 was released.

"My very first recording experience on my own was with a Portastudio. I did a little percussive thing with my voice and a little reverb, and we actually ended up using that on *Station to Station*."

– Carlos Alomar
Songwriter/Musician
(solo, David Bowie, John Lennon)

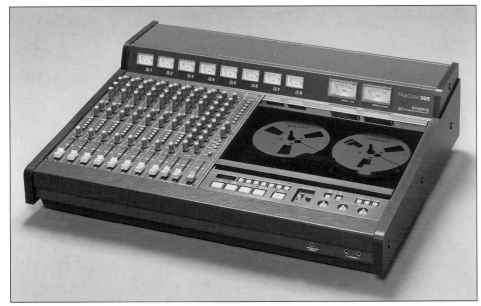

Then and now, nothing looks quite like the sleek TASCAM 388 Studio 8.

"It was one of the first self-contained professional studios that gave you eight tracks on 1/4-inch reels, rather than four tracks on a cassette. All of the 'Cruise the USA in a Chevrolet' commercials, among many others, were produced on a 388."

"The Studio 8 always sounded great and never gave me a minute's trouble," recalls Gene Joly, who sold the machines at E.U. Wurlitzer Music in Boston before joining TASCAM in 1998. "There's a lot of them still in use today. One of our service centers here in L.A. still gets one or two 388s a week in for a checkup, which is amazing because they haven't been built for over a decade. We get the same thing with guys ordering parts for their 20-year old 144s all the time."

TASCAM went on to release a range of products over the next three years to further establish the company in the eyes of pro production studios. The T-Series (T-2620MS, T-2640MS, T-26402S) were TASCAM's first cassette duplicators that got many studios into the tape duplication business, the MS-16 was the company's first 16-track recorder with SMPTE, and the MIDlizer MTS-1000 was a timecode synchronizer/controller that became the heart of countless early SMPTE-based audio studios.

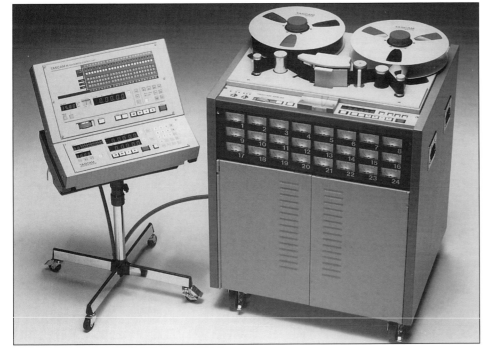

TASCAM's first 2-inch 24-track recorder, the ATR-80/24. The RC-824 controller and AQ-80 auto-locator remote cart could be 30 feet from the recorder without inducing data errors.

"The first product I was involved with directly was the M-2500 Series mixer," says Hildebrandt. "That one really started the boom before Mackie introduced their 8-bus board. It was an updated version of the old Model 5, which then became the Model 35 mixer, and ultimately the M-2500. That was the first modern-day, 8-bus analog board, and it was big news at that point in time."

The MIDIizer was a versatile controller and SMPTE generator that fit any number of music and audio-for-video production suites. Offering MIDI-to-timecode and tape transport synchronization and control, the MTS-1000 was capable of handling ATR-MIDI, ATR-ATR, or VTR-ATR-MIDI system configurations.

The ATR-80/24 and ATR-80/32 were the company's first forays into large-format, 24-track recorders designed with full synchronization support. The ATR-80s were high-performance recorders with +4 dBU inputs and outputs, plug-in circuit cards, and an 8-bit digital-to-analog converter that ensured very short

record and erase bias ramps (53 microseconds at 30 ips) for silent punch-ins and -outs. In an A/B comparison test at Lion Share Studios in Los Angeles, the ATR-80/24's specs and performance kept pace with 24-track recorders from Otari, Studer, and MCI—but only after the ATR had been dusted off from a nasty fall.

"The road case slipped off the truck's lift gate and fell five feet to the pavement outside Lion's Share," winces Jim Lucas. "The screws holding the deck plate were bent at about a 30-degree angle, so we thought the demo would never happen. But when we put up an alignment tape to re-align the machine, it was—amazingly—still in perfect alignment! No other machine on the planet could do that. Just rolling an MCI machine down a hallway would throw those recorders out of alignment, but you could drop an ATR-80 five feet and it would still perform great with machines costing two or three times as much."

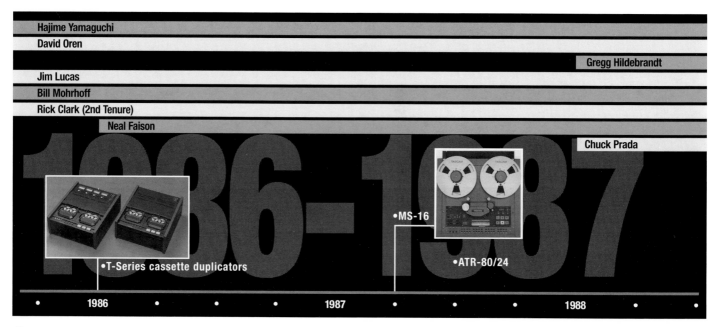

Hajime Yamaguchi
David Oren
Gregg Hildebrandt
Jim Lucas
Bill Mohrhoff
Rick Clark (2nd Tenure)
Neal Faison
Chuck Prada

•T-Series cassette duplicators
•MS-16
•ATR-80/24

1986   1987   1988

How Did They Do That?

The sharp 238 Syncaset was a pleasure to work with and was the first TASCAM product available with Dolby S noise reduction.

The 688 MIDIStudio added sophisticated configuration scene recall, full MIDI and SMPTE control, and an extensive mixer to the Portastudio lineage.

Given the pace the company was setting in multitrack cassette head technology, one would have thought TASCAM could eventually build a 24-track analog Portastudio. Though sixteen tracks short of that pipe dream, the 238 Syncaset nonetheless surprised a lot of people. The 238's high-quality sound and pro features seemed almost too good to be true: a rotary shuttle control, automatic punch-in-out with rehearsal mode, a 3-point auto-locator, remote control, and a serial computer interface that allowed stacked 238s to communicate with external machines via timecode.

"When the 238 came out, everyone said 'You can't put eight tracks on a cassette!'" laughs Chuck Prada. "Just listen to it! It really had a tough start because nobody believed it could be done. Even demonstrating how great it sounded didn't get it to do as well as we wanted it to. That's when the 688 and the 644 came out—the MIDIStudios. Those were complex machines, but they got the 238s selling like hotcakes. Those who got to know the 644 and 688 were able to get some great-sounding projects completed

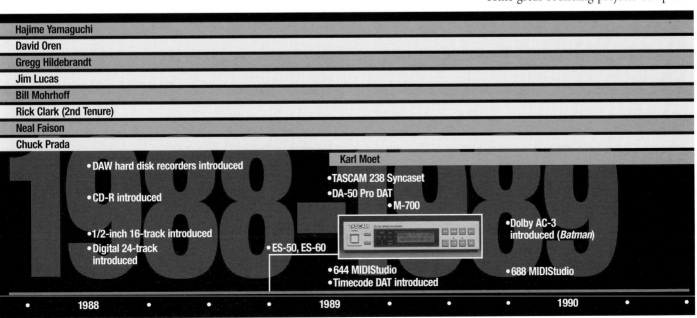

Hajime Yamaguchi
David Oren
Gregg Hildebrandt
Jim Lucas
Bill Mohrhoff
Rick Clark (2nd Tenure)
Neal Faison
Chuck Prada

• DAW hard disk recorders introduced

Karl Moet

• TASCAM 238 Syncaset
• DA-50 Pro DAT
• CD-R introduced
• M-700

• 1/2-inch 16-track introduced
• Digital 24-track introduced
• ES-50, ES-60
• Dolby AC-3 introduced (*Batman*)

• 688 MIDIStudio

• 644 MIDIStudio
• Timecode DAT introduced

1988   1989   1990

on them, and folks who couldn't afford the 688 could buy a 238 and a cheap mixer to round it out."

With the advent of MIDI in 1984, electronic studios began popping up everywhere, thanks to a surge of popular music soaked in synthesis. Re-tooling a new Portastudio that supported the MIDI spec made perfect sense, so TASCAM introduced the 644 MIDIStudio at Winter NAMM in 1989. The 644 featured an 8-channel, 16-input, 4-bus mixer, 4-track cassette recorder, and an LCD screen that provided a detailed view of the unit's 99 mixer "scene" configurations. Fitted with a built-in MIDI tape synchronizer and compatible with TASCAM's MIDIizer, the $1,495 MIDIStudio 644 was used extensively for music and audio-for-video work.

The 688 MIDIStudio was released later in 1989, and upped the ante with a 10-channel, 20-input, 8-bus mixer and an 8-track cassette recorder for $3,299. The 688 also offered an improved scene display section, dbx noise reduction switchable in 4-track groups, an independent 8 x 2 cue monitor section, and a nifty meter bridge.

TASCAM's first large-format mixing console was the M-700. Dubbed "the baby SSL" when an add-on fader package was introduced shortly after its release, the M-700 was a 40 x 32 mixer that retained the familiar feel of a traditional console while performing with the best the high-end competition had to offer.

"After my Portastudio, the next biggie for me was the 8-track 688 MIDIStudio. I cut a lot of stuff with it that we used for a number of records, including Praxis's *Transmutation and* Zillatron's *Lord of the Harvest for* Bootsy's Rubber Band, just to name a few. Thanks for the many years, TASCAM."

– Bootsy Collins
   Bassist/Songwriter
   (solo, P-Funk Allstars,
   George Clinton, Herbie Hancock)

The M-700 was a 40 x 32 mixer that retained the familiar feel of a traditional console while performing with the best the high-end competition had to offer.

The First Legal DAT

> The DAT store was just a phenomenon; word started to spread, and that tiny place on Santa Monica Boulevard did a huge amount of business in grey market DATs.

Initially referred to as an R-DAT (rotary head digital audio tape) machine, TASCAM decided to drop the "R" and simply call it the DA-50 Pro DAT. DAT machines were already being sold stateside in the "gray market" by shops like The DAT Store in Santa Monica, California, but the Recording Industry of America Association (RIAA) was using the courts to keep illegal DAT recorders out of the country for fear of unbridaled digital copies ignoring copyright laws. The solution was the Serial Copy Management System (SCMS): a "copyright-asserted" bit code that prevented more than one digital copy to be made from one DAT tape to another.

"People were excited about this technology and they wanted it, but they couldn't get it," recalls Casey Zygmont. "Everyone knew these machines were available in Japan, so The DAT Store started going to Japan and bringing the machines stateside. That store was just a phenomenon; word started to spread, and that tiny place on Santa Monica Boulevard did a huge amount of business in grey market DATs. We were the first ones prepared to bring legal DATs over once SCMS became the agreed-upon solution."●

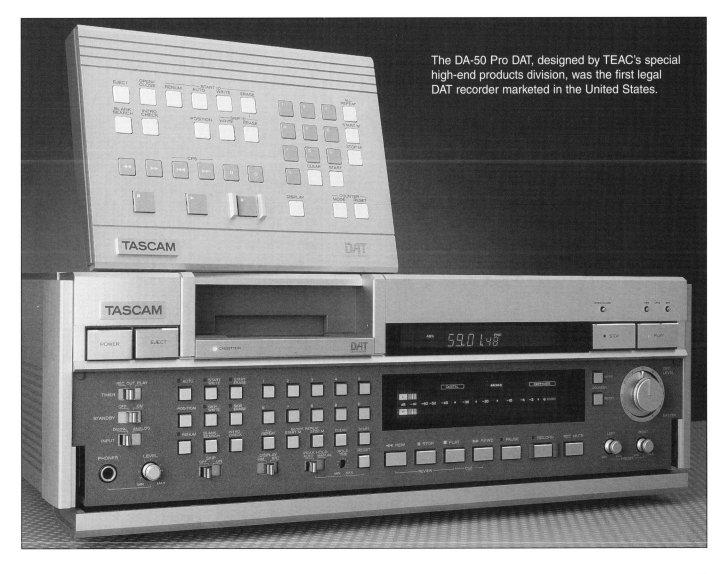

The DA-50 Pro DAT, designed by TEAC's special high-end products division, was the first legal DAT recorder marketed in the United States.

TECHNOLOGY TIMELINE 2 CONT.

THE DIGITAL DECADE: 1990 – 1999

DIGITALLY SPEAKING . A STAR IS BORN . A FRIEND IN POST IS A FRIEND INDEED . IN A FOREST OF DA-88s
THE NEW NUTS AND BOLTS . BACKSTAGE AT THE EMMYS . SAVING A SUBMARINE

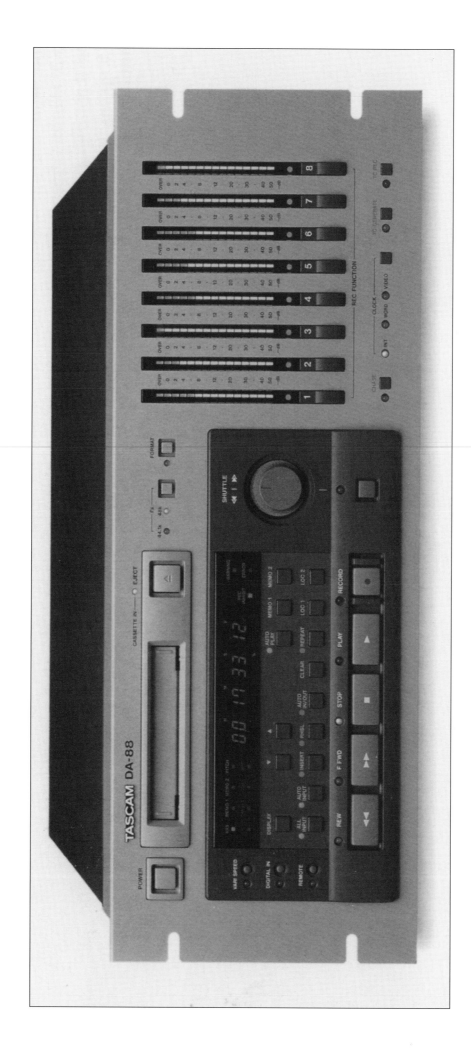

Digitally Speaking

Shown here with the RC-424 remote control and rackmount power unit, the affordable MSR-24 was an ideal entry point into the world of high-capacity multitrack recording.

TASCAM's M-3700 was the first mixer in its class to include dynamic and snapshot automation as standard equipment.

The momentum of TASCAM's innovation boom in the late 1980s paved the way for a pivotal decade of digital excellence. TASCAM and TEAC product engineers were adding 0s and 1s to their design tool belts with the introduction of the DA-50 R-DAT in 1989—the company's product family would never look or sound quite the same again. Having long since shed the "semi-pro" misnomer two decades before, TASCAM continued to build on its leading position in the home recording and musician markets over the next ten years with a flurry of product releases aimed at professional users.

Though setting its sights on the high-end, TASCAM was still passionately devoted to developing analog-based machines, as well. The company's first 1-inch 24-track recorder in 1990 further strengthened TASCAM's commitment to the commercial studio and production markets. Priced at an astonishing $13,999, the MSR-24 was designed for independent musicians and pro music and post-production studios trying to economically upgrade to 24 tracks. Featuring gapless punch-in/-out,

SMPTE/EBU/RS-232 compatability, and Dolby S and dbx Type 1 noise reduction switchable in 8-channel groups, the MSR-24 came as close to the new digital audio of the day as many could get without taking the digital plunge.

The M-3700 carried on the company's M-3500 line of input consoles designed specifically for budget- and space-minded project and commercial studios. Starting at $12,999, the 3700 was a dream for anyone chasing the expensively-elusive Holy Grail of mix-and-signal automation. Built-in fader and signal routing automation was available in dynamic or snapshot modes, and the mixer also sported a disc drive and SMPTE timecode generator/reader. Audio I/O was handled with unbalanced –10 dBv connectors, but TASCAM also offered a +4 dBm balanced input and output option that came with a meter extension bridge for dedicated tape return input, channel input, and auxillary output monitoring needs.

	1990			1991			1992	
Hajime Yamaguchi								
David Oren								
Gregg Hildebrandt								
Jim Lucas								
Bill Mohrhoff								
Rick Clark (2nd Tenure)								
Neal Faison								
Chuck Prada								
Karl Moet								
			Casey Zygmont					

ADAT introduced at AES/New York •

TASCAM
TEAC Professional Division

• DA-30

• MSR-24
• DA-800/24 DASH
• M-3700
• DA-P20

Perhaps no machine characterized TASCAM's drive to reach the upper echelons of audio production more than its DA-800/24 digital recorder. Created through a cooperative development effort with Sony and Panasonic, TASCAM's 800 employed the Digital Audio Stationary Head (DASH) format, and was fully compatible with Sony's industry-standard PCM-3324 and 3324A digital formats. Featuring 24 digital and two analog channels, and a dump-edit function for manual tape slicing, the 800 also took advantage of TEAC's ZD circuitry in its A/D and D/A converters to suppress low-level distortion.

The DA-50 was on every engineer's wish list in 1990, too; but at $5,000 it was a pricey leap for all but a few before the ensuing RIAA agreement that opened the door for legal DATs to enter the country. No longer "gray market" machines, DAT recorders instantly became the 2-track mastering deck of choice. Building on the DA-50's technological advances, it didn't take long for TASCAM's DA-30 to achieve "industry standard" status with professional studio owners. Its $1,899 price tag allowed studios to buy multiple

machines while making DAT technology a first-time reality for independent musicians, as well.

The compact size of DAT tapes made the recorders a natural for remote recording applications. TEAC's first portable was the DA-P20: a lightweight unit that was easy to grab when recording in the field. Sound designers instantly adopted the DA-P20 for capturing and retrieving remote sounds; enough to cause the first production run to sell out practically overnight. The recorder had S/PDIF I/O, balanced XLR mic/line inputs with –20 dB pad, 16-bit linear converters, and could record for up to two hours on its rechargeable battery pack. TASCAM followed up the recorder's success with the DA-P1 portable DAT in 1994—designed for professional remote recordists.

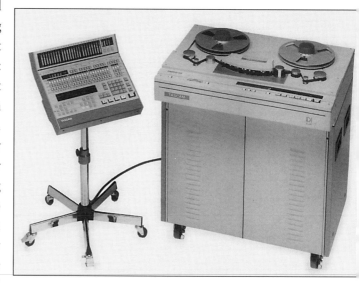

The DA-800/24 DASH was TASCAM's first multitrack digital recorder.

The affordable DA-30 DAT recorder brought digital audio into countless home, studio, and post-production rooms for the first time.

A Star Is Born

"There's a creative and a

technological rush you get with

new equipment. One is the

excitement of the creative process

and having your music come to

life; the other is to gain technical

knowledge with the gear you're

using to make your hard work

come to fruition. Experiencing

both processes simultaneously

is very exciting."

– Willie Wilcox

Drummer/Producer/Sound

Designer (Utopia, Todd Rundgren,

Hall & Oates, Meat Loaf, Natalie

Cole, Luther Vandross, Sci-Fi

Channel, USA Networks)

The 1990s ushered in a new era of digital TASCAM technology, and the undisputed star of the show, from its opening night, was the legendary DA-88 Digital Multitrack System. The DA-88 was a perfect stepping-stone into the future of digital recording technology for a company that had practically re-invented analog recording since 1969—and it couldn't have come at a more crucial time. Analog was still alive and well, but the advent of affordable DAT machines and digital recorders took more than a little wind out of reel-to-reel analog sales. Considering the audio climate of 1990, it's fair to say the DA-88, which won an

Emmy just 18 months after its introduction (see p.12, *Awards Chart*), was single-handedly responsible for both kick-starting and ultimately skyrocketing TASCAM to its leading role in the audio world today.

Initially designed in response to a new breed of modular multitrack digital recorders, the DA-88 took full advantage of TEAC's head, drive, and aeronautical engineering expertise. Alesis had announced its S-VHS-based ADAT at AES-New York in September 1991 to rave reviews, but units weren't actually shipped for over a year. TASCAM's

Like the Portastudio in 1979, just about every musician, producer, and commercial studio has used a DA-88.

Hajime Yamaguchi

Gregg Hildebrandt

Chuck Prada

Jim Lucas

Bill Mohrhoff

Rick Clark (2nd Tenure)

Neal Faison

Karl Moet

Casey Zygmont

•Sony SDDS introduced (*Last Action Hero*)

•MD recorders introduced

DA-88 introduced AES/San Francisco•

•Dolby Digital introduced

DTS discrete 5.1 introduced (*Jurassic Park*)•

| 1992 | 1993 | 1994 |

"We pushed it hard, but lots of people in the post industry wanted the DA-88 to succeed as much, if not more, than we did."

designers first opted for TEAC's existing head and drive mechanisms in order to rush the DA-88 to market in that span of time, but soon recognized the real value in plying the same components in the DA-88 that the space shuttle uses in every mission.

"TEAC's Airborne Division makes a flight data recorder," says Jim Lucas. "It's based on an 8-millimeter rotary head transport and is on board every space shuttle that's ever flown. NASA wanted a device that would survive a 9g impact, so TEAC ruggedized a recorder they built for the Air Force and NATO and put it to the test. NASA said, 'My God, we only needed to be able to salvage the data from it—we didn't expect it to still work!' That is the same transport in the DA-88, and that's why it's such a reliable product."

The DA-88's impact on the post-production industry was immediate and profound. Built-in synchronization and a rugged transport made it the perfect transition for studios moving from analog to digital post-production tools. TASCAM's engineering team was able to respond instantly to minor glitches that arose in the unit's first six months of production; a fact that endeared the company and its products to post engineers and facility owners alike. In fact, some say the latter almost wanted the DA-88 to come to market more than the former.

"We pushed it hard, but lots of people in the post industry wanted the DA-88 to

succeed as much, if not more, than we did," Lucas continues. "Studio owners saw how much money they could save with it, and engineers liked the built-in synchronization and ease of transporting tapes between studios; so the DA-88 quickly became the international exchange currency between production facilities. Before the DA-88, sending tapes to other studios required that they have the exact same dubber or tape machine with a specific Dolby card setup that matched your own. This limited production work to a handful of high-end facilities, but the DA-88 changed all that. Today, just put an 8mm tape in a FedEx envelope, and it can play back the next morning at just about any studio in the world. It must be said, though, that the DA-88 would not have been nearly this successful if it weren't for the massive amount of feedback and help we received from the Chuck Garshas, Chuck Pells, and Jay Palmers of the post-production world."

The DA-88 first starred in 1993 at an AES show in one of the Hyatt Hotel's conference rooms. Having arrived from Japan just days before the unveiling, the prototype was locked away in a secure room with little more than a light bulb working inside it. Gregg Hildebrandt was given the unveiling honors, and recalls a changing industry at that time; not to mention the months of break-neck road trips to follow.

"We were pretty dedicated to analog at that time," says Hildebrandt, "but we knew the next wave of digital recorders

"A Friend in Post Is a Friend Indeed"

TASCAM's Production Products Group Manager since 1985, Jim Lucas applied his background in theater technology, studio design, sales, and synchronizer manufacturing to the DA-88 like never before. Before coming to TASCAM, he designed a couple of studios in Hollywood and Rome, was Sony's Western Regional Sales Manager, and worked for BTX—the first synchronizer manufacturer—in the late '70s and early '80s. Miking announcer Vin Scully at Los Angeles Dodger home games upon first moving to California, Lucas recalls two markets primed for the new Hi-8 recorder.

"The DA-88 grew out of a need to respond to the ADAT, which was a very significant product introduction," Lucas says. "It took not only us, but the entire industry pretty much by surprise; but we didn't want to simply build a response to the ADAT. Based on our experience in synchronizing open-reel decks in post-production studios, we decided to add every conceivable synchronization hook we could think of to the machine. That's what eventually got the DA-88 into Hollywood film, video, and post studios."

The TASCAM product line had already been used for years in broadcast, and particularly, in radio, for its cost-effectiveness, rugged engineering, and the fact that it all could be modified to work in broadcast environments for far less than the cost of buying custom broadcast equipment. "The same was true for television and film production use, but we didn't get into that marketplace until the advent of the DA-88," Lucas continues. "I took one look at that machine and told the engineers that what they were designing was going to take the production world by storm. There was no other machine on the market that could do what it did. TEAC wanted it for the music market, but we thought we'd only get the upper-end music guys to buy it—that it was going to instead take over post-production. As it turns out, it looks like I was pretty much right on with that, though the machine eventually went on to do quite well in music,

continued next page

was just around the corner. The main question for us with the DA-88 was in deciding whether to go after the music or post markets with it first, because we didn't have the resources to try and service both in the beginning. We received three DA-88 pre-production samples, and proceeded to book dealer seminars, user clinics, and store events day and night for the next four months solid. The problem was, we had nothing to ship; so six of us, including Bill Mohrhoff, Chuck Prada, Karl Moet, and myself took

these units and were handing them off in airports to each other to get them out to these clinics as fast as we could. Dealers thought there must have been hundreds of DA-88s out there, but we were just criss-crossing the country with these same three units! Remarkably, those machines never once broke down."

The original DA-88, introduced at AES in San Francisco by Gregg Hildebrandt, was initially going to be called the MDR-88.

Hajime Yamaguchi			
Gregg Hildebrandt			
Chuck Prada			
Jim Lucas			
		Bill Mohrhoff (2nd Tenure)	
Rick Clark (2nd Tenure)			
Neal Faison			
Karl Moet			
Casey Zygmont			
Roger Maycock			

•DDA-P1

•DA-88 wins Emmy award

1994   1995   1996

In a Forest of DA-88s

"I can't tell you how many projects I've worked on that started from tracks people have done on DA-88s, and before that even on Portastudios. I mixed a track for U2 a few years ago, a version of the Beatles' 'Happiness Is a Warm Gun,' and they supplied us with about forty-eight tracks of drum tapes, vocal takes, and bass parts; all on DA-88 tapes."

– Joe Chiccarelli
  Grammy-winning
  Producer/Engineer
  (Beck, Etta James,
  U2, Tori Amos)

Lucas was guiding the company's early DA-88 efforts when a severe back injury put him on the disabled list just as the first DA-88s were reaching the docks in San Pedro Harbor. With a lot of help from a recuperating product groups manager stuck at home, Gregg Hildebrandt found out who and where all the important bodies were at the industry's top film, television, post, audio, and video groups, and wore Lucas's hat for the next year.

"I found the engineers wanted the DA-88 to work even more than we did," laughs Hildebrandt. "They were locked into various DASH or Pro Digi machines that really didn't work well in particular environments. These were the same young engineers that grew up cutting their teeth on the 80-8s and such, so they were already very comfortable with TASCAM. It became pretty obvious to us where the initial market was going to be."

A number of top audio dealers in the L.A. basin were pivotal to TASCAM's instant success with the DA-88, including

"A Friend in Post Is a Friend Indeed," *continued*

as well. It all goes back to our engineering staff, which is superb."

"The DA-88 fit in as a transition between old mag film and the new server streaming systems," continues Lucas. "It was a great bridge that got them away from the mag and having to align Dolby units. It increased their efficiency, and cut tape and storage costs, and was just a wonderful device to get people over that hump. The DA-88 got them out of one format and into the digital domain, but it wasn't perfect. They couldn't do edits or slip tracks, and it was only 16-bit, so there was still a noise floor problem and some dynamic range issues. Mag with Dolby SR gives you incredible dynamic range; much more than 16-bit

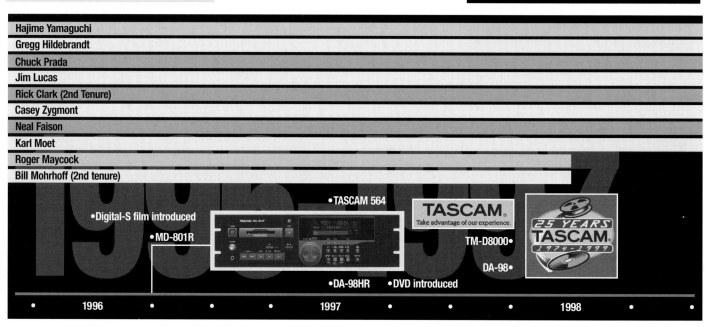

Hajime Yamaguchi
Gregg Hildebrandt
Chuck Prada
Jim Lucas
Rick Clark (2nd Tenure)
Casey Zygmont
Neal Faison
Karl Moet
Roger Maycock
Bill Mohrhoff (2nd tenure)

•Digital-S film introduced
  •MD-801R
  •TASCAM 564
  •DA-98HR   •DVD introduced

TASCAM.
Take advantage of our experience.

25 YEARS
TASCAM.
1974-1999

TM-D8000•

DA-98•

1996   1997   1998

"We filled up the entire building around the sales desks; it was like a forest of DA-88s!"

digital. We knew it wasn't the answer for everybody, but it got our name and our faces and our personnel into their hearts and minds, and I think we've done an excellent job of servicing the industry."

Everything Audio, Professional Audio Services, and Audio Intervisual Design (AID). The latter was a Sony dealer at the time the DA-88 was introduced, and very well-connected with Hollywood's television and post facilities. TASCAM was still largely an MI company and didn't have much to offer AID until Jeff Evans saw the DA-88 and knew it would sell to post. TASCAM still wanted to go after the music market with the new recorder, but eventually opened up AID and other post dealers. Just six month later, the DA-88 had replaced Otari's MTR-90 as the standard audio recorder in all post studios.

AID went on to become the top DA-88 dealer on the West Coast, but only after some serious inventory control. Working closely with the Disneys and Paramounts of the world, AID was ordering and shipping enough units per day to effectively choke the daylight out of their small facility on La Brea Avenue in Hollywood.

"DA-88s were stacked everywhere," recalls Casey Zygmont. "We filled up the entire building around the sales desks; it was like a forest of DA-88s! Post engineers liked the small tape size, but mainly they liked it because it was modular. They could do the various parts of a production on separate tapes and send one to an editing suite, put ADR on another, sound effects and Foley on a third, and then bring it all together on the mix stage. Entire productions were traditionally done on one MTR-90 2-inch master reel that had to be bounced from suite to suite; with the DA-88, they instead had five tiny master tapes that could go anywhere."

EFX Studios in Burbank changed hands and the new owner immediately ordered 40 DA-88s, and Universal Studios was buying up 25, 30, 40, or more machines at a time. Doing sound design for one of the *Star Trek* movies when the DA-88 was first introduced, Skywalker South on Bundy Street used to rent extra DA-88s from places like Studio Instrument Rentals every time they ran out of tracks.

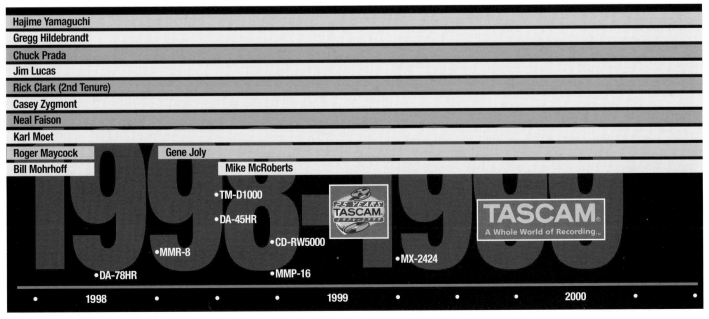

Hajime Yamaguchi
Gregg Hildebrandt
Chuck Prada
Jim Lucas
Rick Clark (2nd Tenure)
Casey Zygmont
Neal Faison
Karl Moet
Roger Maycock   Gene Joly
Bill Mohrhoff   Mike McRoberts

• TM-D1000
• DA-45HR
• CD-RW5000
• MMR-8
• MX-2424
• DA-78HR   • MMP-16

25 YEARS TASCAM
TASCAM® A Whole World of Recording™

1998   1999   2000

The New Nuts and Bolts

TEAC had years of experience building data recorders and drive mechanisms around the Hi-8 tape. The format was shuttle-worthy, and had been used to film the smart bomb flight paths that ran continuously on CNN during Desert Storm; but Hi-8 was completely new to those capturing audio. TEAC had built VHS-based recorders for years, but stopped making the drives by the time the ADAT was released; so the company opted for the newer 8mm technology with the DA-88.

"You could do more with 8mm than VHS," says Casey Zygmont. "It was a longer tape that could hold one hundred minutes of audio, and it was a much newer technology that was developed in the mid '80s—whereas VHS had been around since the '70s. TEAC used the same 8mm drive and transport in the black box airborne video recorders, communication recorders, and in the DA-88. It's a very rugged mechanism."

The DA-88's arrival to the market was delayed because the company wanted it to be a synchronizable deck, and TASCAM knew it would also be hard to match the ADAT dollar-for-dollar. The latter used off-the-shelf parts for its transport to keep production costs low, so entering the high-end post market first with the DA-88 looked like the best route for TASCAM to take.

"We knew the DA-88's sync capabilities in the long run were going to be pretty important to us," says Gregg Hildebrandt. "We also knew the price sensitivity was going to be critical if we tried to sell the DA-88 for the same price as the ADAT. We could have brought the DA-88 in at the same price as the ADAT for about a week, but we knew Alesis would drop the price as soon as we started shipping our units because they had such a huge margin in the original ADAT. It didn't make any sense for us to get into that price battle, so we sold the DA-88 into an area they couldn't go after."

Roger Maycock started working for TASCAM just after the DA-88 was shipped. "We ended up with a tape format that was relatively inexpensive," says Maycock, "and a rapid response transport mechanism that was able to meet the synchronization needs of the post-production market. The DA-88 has become a standard in post-production for doing mix stems in film and television, and it's enjoying a new wave of popularity as a great mixdown medium for surround sound work."

"I have six DA-88s in the U.K., and I do a lot of transferring of audio on the 8mm tapes. It's very easy to go from one tape to another with the DA-88, and it's far more flexible than any reel-to-reel format. For the *Time Machine*, the guitarist, drummer, and percussionist each recorded some of their parts and patterns on their DA-88s at home."

– Alan Parsons
  Producer/Engineer/Artist (Beatles, Pink Floyd, Hollies, Paul McCartney, Alan Parsons Project)

The format was shuttle-worthy and had been used to film the smart bomb flight paths that ran continuously on CNN during Desert Storm; but Hi-8 was completely new to those capturing audio.

"Backstage at the Emmys"

Roger Maycock evolved from Product Specialist to Marcom Support Manager and back again in his four-year tenure with TASCAM. A musician and school band director before joining the company on June 1, 1994, he added another title to his TASCAM resume soon after: Emmy Podium Spokesperson.

"I nominated the DA-88 for a technical award in 1995 because everyone at Paramount, Fox, Universal, and NBC were using the things," says Maycock. "Three months later, TASCAM won the Emmy; they've won another for technical achievement with the MMR-8 and MMP-16, and now a Science and Engineering Academy plaque. TASCAM has had a very fond place in my heart ever since I bought my first Model 38 and 32. I did a lot of electronic music with those two, and eventually wondered how I could make a living working with all this new gear. That's when I joined Roland, and ultimately the folks at TASCAM."

"Bill Mohrhoff taught me a lot," credits Maycock. "He showed me the aspects of the business as a PR and marcom person; what needed to be done to keep in constant touch with the press to schedule product reviews, place

continued next page

Jim Lucas and Universal Studios' David "Doc" Goldstein behind a rack of MMR-8s and MMP-16s.

Saving a Submarine

TASCAM talked to everyone in the film and television post studios before building the company's first disk-based digital multitrack recorder and modular audio player. Though happy with the DA-88, users wanted the ability to slip tracks and edit audio on the mix stage, and avoiding 20-minute wait times when transferring DA-88 reels was another high priority. Post studios typically wait for a new technology to be time-tested before using it, but once they do, it's a major commitment for every room in the house.

The MMR-8 and MMP-16 duo recently added another Emmy to TASCAM's trophy case—the first time any audio company has won two awards in such a short span of time—and the MMR-8 received an Academy Award for "discoveries or inventions of special and outstanding value to the arts and sciences of motion pictures," just as this book went to press. In a world of audio formats, the ability to edit and play back all of them on the TASCAM tandem allows the likes of Disney, Warner Brothers, and Fox to work with any composer, dialog house, or Foley room without conflict.

"We wanted the ability to tell post engineers, 'Give us your disk, and we'll plug it in and play it back without transfers, so you can get back to work,'" Lucas says. "We got rid of the necessity to do tape transfers. We had a recent situation where Universal was finishing up a major motion picture. Somebody had cut in a different scene that didn't match the soundtrack just hours before they were supposed to go to final print master, and everyone's panicking except

it's a small-budget production," Lucas continues. "Universal used thirty-two DA-88s just for the temp dub of the sound effects on one major motion picture. The ability to fix something on the fly with the MMR-8 is more critical to sound editors than the transfer time it saves them."

The company released its first 2-track MiniDisc recorder in 1996: the MD-801R. Marketed as a flexible alternative to tape-based systems, the 801 featured a

"Backstage at the Emmys," continued

press releases, and to follow that all up to make sure the materials were getting out there. The skills that I developed during those years at TASCAM have been extremely important to my own business today."

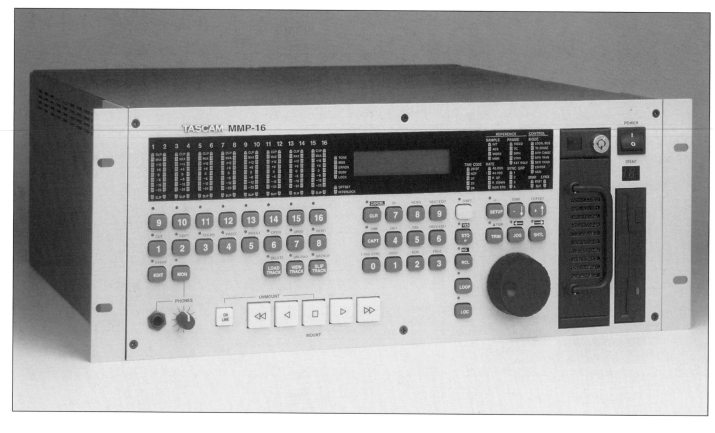

the mixers running the session. In the old days, it would've taken hours, if not days, to send the reels out and get them back; but these two mixers fixed the problem and saved the project in a matter of minutes."

How much time is saved on an average production with the MMP-16? "On a *Waterworld*, it could be thousands of hours, or at least a few hundred hours if

jog/shuttle dial, XLR audio inputs and outputs, and a wide pitch control range of ±9.9% that appealed to sample-based dance studios. The MiniDisc format didn't match up with DAT, but the MD-801 provided enough pro features to give any serious recording enthusiast the tools they needed for audio editing. The company released the TASCAM 564 the following year—the world's first MiniDisc digital multitracker.

The MMP-16 Modular Multitrack Player, one half of TASCAM's Emmy-awarded post-production tandem.

The company released the TASCAM 564 the following year—the world's first MiniDisc digital multitracker.

"Ben and I both bought DA-88s for our second Ben Folds Five record. We got the record company to buy our tape machines as part of the budget, and we recorded the record ourselves. It was really liberating because we could both record at home and then combine our ideas in the studio."

– Robert Sledge

Bassist/Songwriter

(Ben Folds Five)

Using the same Hi-8 format as the DA-88, the DA-98 was also introduced in 1997. A more sophisticated version of the DA-88, the DA-98 offered confidence monitoring for playback and live recording, and was designed with the high-end video post market in mind. Enhanced 18-bit A/D and D/A converters and a built-in SMPTE/MIDI/9-pin synchronizer were added, and the 98 was backwards-compatible with DA-88 and DA-38 tapes.

The company's first digital mixer, the TM-D8000, came out that same year, and offered high-end users a potent tandem when used with the DA-98. The 8000 wasn't affordable for budget-conscious studios, but TASCAM soon served that market with the popular TM-D1000. The 1000, which featured built-in snapshot automation and effects processing, was the world's first sub-$1,000 mixer that allowed many studios to get their first taste of clean digital mixing. The DA-45HR, released in 1998 as the world's first 24-bit R-DAT recorder, and still popular today, won recording innovation awards from *Pro Audio Review*, *Studio Sound*, and *Keyboard* magazines shortly after its introduction.

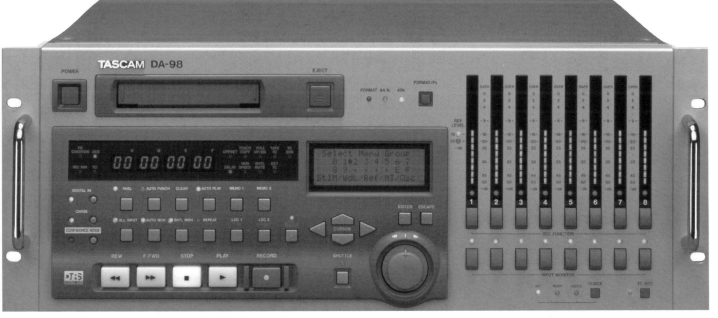

Targeted for sophisticated video post houses, TASCAM's DA-98 was a significant update to the DA-88.

Another Strong Finish

TASCAM closed out the 1990s with a flurry of product releases that set the stage for another new millennium of innovation. Recordable and rewritable CDs were replacing DAT and 2-track reel-to-reel tapes as the mixdown medium of choice for many, and the dream of affordable 24-bit random access recording was becoming a reality.

Following the release of its first computer CD burner bundles in 1998, TASCAM further developed the exploding CD-R market with a slew of recorders. The $1,299 CD-RW5000 was TASCAM's first standalone CD-R and CD-RW recorder, and the Mac- and PC-based CD-R624 CD burner/software bundle offered the first tool that allowed users to create MP3 files for audio delivery over the Web. The CD-D4000 personal CD duplicator was introduced at the same time.

TASCAM's next addition to its popular DTRS-formatted recorder family was the DA-78HR, the first modular digital multitracker to bring pristine 24-bit performance in to many studios. The DA-78HR featured built-in timecode capabilities, S/PDIF I/O, and an internal mixer with level and pan for bouncing tracks or creating spot mixdowns directly from the unit.

The company's final major product release of the '90s was the revolutionary MX-2424 (pictured below-top). Introduced at AES in September 1999, the MX-2424 closed out TASCAM's digital decade as the world's first affordable 24-track, 24-bit hard disk recorder ever created. Its combination of high-resolution recording, editing capabilities, and timecode-generating and chasing features for just $3,999, made the MX-2424 an instant winner with project and professional studios; and its ability to automatically write WAV and Sound Designer II audio files made it a perfect companion for computer-based facilities.●

> "What's wonderful is that the company makes professional audio gear at an affordable price. As TASCAM has grown electronically, we've grown with them."
>
> – George Duke
> Producer/Artist (solo, Dizzy Gillespie, Cannonball Adderly, Frank Zappa, Clarke/Duke Project, Dianne Reeves)

Another TASCAM innovation, the DA-78HR was the world's first 24-bit modular digital multitrack machine.

TECHNOLOGY TIMELINE 2 CONT.
'00 AND BEYOND

SAME AS IT EVER WAS . THAT 2340 CHANGED EVERYTHING . TEAM FUTURE
WHAT A DIFFERENCE A PORTASTUDIO MAKES . THE FUTURE IS SO BRIGHT

Same As It Ever Was

"That 2340 Changed Everything"

Gene Joly and TASCAM broke into the music scene at the same time. Before eventually becoming President of E.U. Wurlitzer in Boston, he recalls the time a TEAC 2340 changed his life, and draws parallels to the DJs and rockers of today. "Today's DJ market is very dynamic in terms of creative energy," says Joly. "It reminds me a lot of the early days of rock and roll, so from a cultural perspective, I knew it was going to be a fun industry to get involved with. Just like rock in the late '60s, the rules are being made up as we go along."

continued page 71

A lot has changed since TASC formed in Tokyo, Dr. Abe modified a 4010 in Marina Del Rey, and TASCAM joined the TEAC family in Montebello. The likes of Lennon, Bowie, Hancock, Springsteen, Cobain, and Reznor have created their music while TASCAM was creating the world's first 1/2-inch multitrack, Portastudio, R-DAT, 24-bit R-DAT, Hi-8, MiniDisc multitrack, and 24-track/24-bit hard disk recorders. Add DJs, computer recordists, Web composers, and a scratchable CD deck to those lists, and there's no telling what heights TASCAM may reach in the next 25 years. Having recently posted the biggest month in company history, it's sure to be a long ride.

Change indeed, but TASCAM has been here before. The grass roots DJ market is booming with TASCAM technology, new formats are replacing old ones, and the Portastudio just got a facelift—sounds a lot like 1979. Affordably professional gear was the company's strong suit, then and now, and every focus group, phone call, and user e-mail over the past 25 years has reflected that same need. Whether it was David Oren talking with musicians, Jim Lucas listening to post engineers, or Mike McRoberts chilling with DJs, the call for great-sounding machines has always been heard loud and clear at TASCAM.

"My product development philosophy is to ask people what they want, and then give it to them," says McRoberts. "We had DJs remixing and scratching for us here to see what they want, and one thing they talked about was beat matching: slowing

> "My product development philosophy is to ask people what they want, and then give it to them."

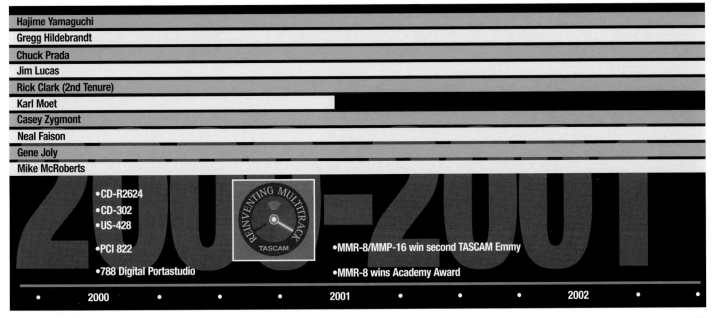

| Hajime Yamaguchi |
| Gregg Hildebrandt |
| Chuck Prada |
| Jim Lucas |
| Rick Clark (2nd Tenure) |
| Karl Moet |
| Casey Zygmont |
| Neal Faison |
| Gene Joly |
| Mike McRoberts |

- •CD-R2624
- •CD-302
- •US-428
- •PCI 822
- •788 Digital Portastudio

REINVENTING MULTITRACK
TASCAM

•MMR-8/MMP-16 win second TASCAM Emmy

•MMR-8 wins Academy Award

| 2000 | 2001 | 2002 |

down a record to match a tempo. I said 'What if you could do that automatically?,' and they thought that would be killer. So I wrote a spec and we came out with the CD-302—the first CD player that did that—and it's the first one they could scratch on. That turned out to be the hit about the machine at that year's DJ Expo, but we never thought this product would supplant vinyl. We want to be big in the DJ market, and this gives us a good start to a whole suite of DJ products."

TASCAM's first personal computer-based recording tools have also dawned in the new millenium, thanks to a partnership with Frontier Design Group. The US-428 is a USB controller for Windows and Macintosh digital audio environments that's relieved a lot of mouse-worn recordists since the first units shipped in mid-2000. Compatible with most major DAW programs, the US-428 provides dedicated controllers for all fader, transport, EQ, mute, solo, aux send/return, transport, and edit parameters, and channels MIDI and analog and S/PDIF audio I/O via USB without installing a sound card. Steinberg's Cubasis VST software is bundled with the 428 thanks to another TASCAM partnership.

The 24-bit PCI 822 is another joint venture with Frontier. TASCAM's first entry into the PCI recording card market features Wordclock synchronization and

A mouse-killer, the US-428 Mac and Windows USB software controller was co-developed with Frontier Design Group.

"That 2340
Changed Everything" *continued*

It took Joly six months after joining TASCAM in 1998 to recruit Mike McRoberts as his International Product Development Manager. "Most everything had been done in Japan before, but we recognized that the world of recording had just too many technologies for any one company to master alone. There were a number that TASCAM had already mastered, and others that we were going to have to partner with other companies in order to bring the best product possible to market in a reasonable period of time. There has to be the right mix of engineering talent on both teams, similar philosophies, and most of all, a chemistry between the two companies. It's worked out really well with Timeline, Frontier Design Group, and several other new partners."

analog, S/PDIF, MIDI, and eight channels of TDIF I/O. Yet another partnership has bundled the PCI 822 with the Gigasampler LE hard disk sampling software from Nemesys; TASCAM having purchased the latter and adding the popular GigaStudio and GigaSampler products to the family.

Filling out TASCAM's Y2K product family are two digital recorders for the high-end post and project recording studio markets. An updated version of the DA-98, the DA-98HR has added AES-EBU and Wordclock I/O, records eight tracks at 48 kHz, four at 96 kHz, or full 192 kHz fidelity on two channels, and can now slave to DTRS remotes or external mechanisms via its serial 9-pin connector; and the MX2424 is the world's first affordable hard disk recorder for musicians.

TASCAM's first integrated hard disk recorder/mixer/multi-effector looks like a spaceship; but even a Model 144 owner will recognize the simplicity in its name: the 788 Digital Portastudio. Over one million Portastudio varieties have been sold since 1979; and for about the same price of its predecessor, the 788 puts more at the musician's fingertips than ever before for $1,149. Eight tracks of uncompressed 24-bit audio, 250 virtual tracks, 999 levels of undo/redo, S/PDIF, MIDI, and a built-in SCSI port for external CD burners may sound daunting

to a 144 user, but the intuitive silver 788 makes it easy to trade in their cassettes for a hard drive when taking the digital plunge.

"The ability for DJs to scratch a CD like we can on vinyl has been on the wish list for a long time; a 'what if' type of thing that's now a reality. It's opened the eyes of a lot of pure turntablists, and taken CD mixing to a whole new level; but it's not trying to replace vinyl scratching. People still used acoustic guitars on stage when solid bodies were introduced, and it's the same thing with vinyl and CDs."

– DJ Davey Dave
  (Überzone, BT,
  Simply Jeff, DJ Spooky)

TASCAM's first integrated hard disk recorder/mixer/multi-effector looks like a spaceship; but even a Model 144 owner will recognize the simplicity in its name: the 788 Digital Portastudio.

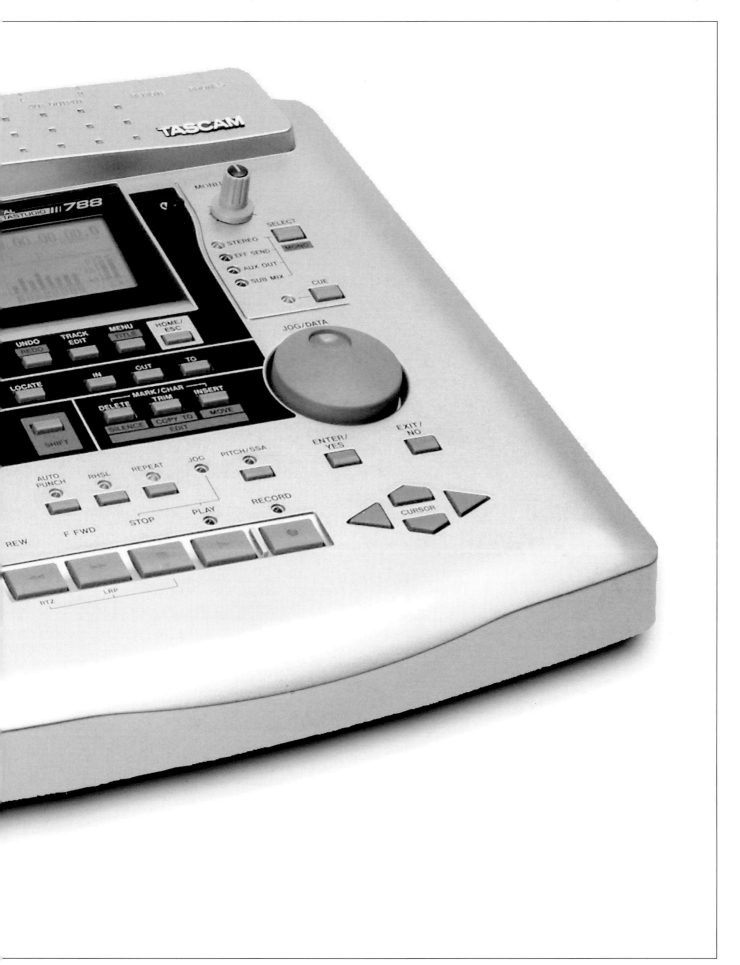

Team Future

"TASCAM is ensuring that their products will integrate into a variety of production environments at a multitude of levels…"

TEAC's collaboration with Sony on the U-matic format videotape recorder in 1966, and TASCAM's co-development with Sony and Panasonic in creating the DASH-compliant DA-800/24 in 1991, set the stage for the company's current wealth of engineering partners. No company can create compatibilty on its own, so TASCAM is teaming with a wide range of partners to build tools for computers, post houses, home studios, and the Web.

"There are more cooperative agreements between firms at all levels of the industry," says Roger Maycock. "We're seeing it in healthcare, and the airline and auto industries, because no one company can afford to be an island unto themselves in this day and age. TASCAM is ensuring that their products will integrate into a variety of production environments at a multitude of levels—from high-level post-production pros all the way down to computer recordists who are buying something like the US-428. That's a broad range of compatibility."

Gregg Hildebrandt agrees. "We wouldn't have formed the alliance with Timeline for the MMR-8 and MMP-16 without first going after the high-end business with the DA-88," he says. "Without that partnership, the MX-2424 would have never happened. The US-428 is another great example of effective partnering with a good engineering company."

"Wow! The first classic piece of TASCAM gear I had was the first 4-track Portastudio. That thing allowed me to put so many classic P-Funk song ideas down that I can't even count 'em. It was such a workhorse, and I still have it to this very day. Nowadays I'm using the DA-78HR 24-bit, and my next move is to get the MX-2424 recorder."

– Bootsy Collins
  Bassist/Songwriter
  (solo, P-Funk Allstars,
  George Clinton, Herbie Hancock)

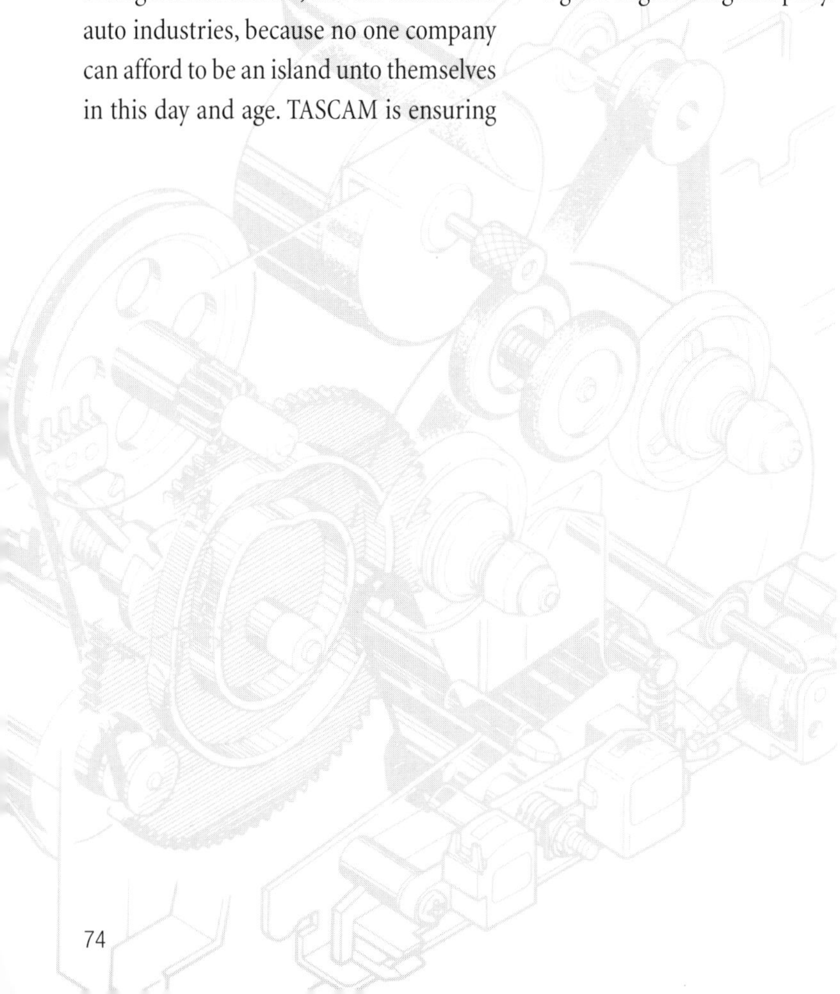

"What a Difference a Portastudio Makes"

Mike McRoberts became TASCAM's International Product Development Manager twenty years after selling his first Portastudio (see photo, p.34) Stopping by Akai, E-mu, and Digidesign along the way before coming aboard in 1998 to spec out the MX-2424, he likes how the next twenty years are shaping up, too.

"The industry's traditionally slow in summer, but we just had our biggest month in TASCAM history," says McRoberts. "It's a great time to be here. I've worked for a lot of great companies, but it's so exciting here right now. We're diversifying; they back us 100% in Tokyo, and we have the freedom to make things happen with a lot of innovative products. TEAC said to come up with all these great products, and it's like we're on this rocketship. We had no product specialists two years ago, and now we have seven; and we now have our own U.S. R&D group in Palo Alto. We've got a lot of work to do, but we have a great time doing it."

The Future Is So Bright

In 1999, TASCAM opened a software research and development center on the northern peninsula of Silicon Valley. Located on the first floor of TEAC's Merlin Engineering Division building, the well-staffed team at PARC (Palo Alto Research Center) are developing core TASCAM technologies and products that should emerge sometime in 2001 and 2002. Some of those technologies will carry on TASCAM's day-one mission of bringing state-of-the-art music and recording products into the home studio.

"If you look at what's missing in the home studio now in terms of affordability, power, and user interface, you can kind of guess what we're working on now," says Gene Joly. "Look at our heritage and the cutting-edge technologies we've created, and you can get a feel for what TASCAM is going to be introducing over the next year."

"The synergy between the individuals at TASCAM is great," says Jim Lucas. "When I started here it was Bill Mohrhoff, Gregg Hildebrandt, Dave Oren, myself, and Mr. Chang—who's been with us forever and is respected by all in the industry. We all wore so many hats in those days, and that team spirit is still here. We had a really close core group of people, and today I think it's even more dynamic. We've broadened our staff considerably to four or five times as many people now in-house, but we still draw on each other's strengths in this environment."

"I'm a TASCAM kind of guy because the gear is easy to use; that's the key for me. Their stuff has always been so user-friendly, and I've never had any mechanical problems with any TASCAM equipment I've owned or used."

– Jim Keltner Drummer/Songwriter/Engineer (Bob Dylan, John Lennon, George Harrison, Neil Young, Ry Cooder, and a member of the Traveling Wilburys)

Lucas sees an audio future with TASCAM front and center. "I see the industry going to network appliance recording equipment in post. You'll take a box and plug it into a hole in the wall, and all of a sudden you're sharing storage media, plug-ins—everything on some sort of network. I think you're going to see more appliances that do more varied things, and fewer appliances that do only one thing. The days of building a physical recorder may be kind of limited. I think a recorder may be built into something that also does multiple things, or the recorder may actually be offsite and accessed with a laser."

"We all wore so many hats in those days, and that team spirit is still here. We had a really close core group of people, and today I think it's even more dynamic."

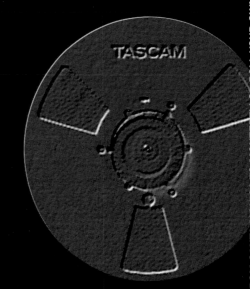

A RECORDING 3
REVOLUTION
BY DESIGN

ADS AND MARKETING

SPEAKING MUSICIANESE . FROM SANTA MONICA TO MONTEBELLO . ROLL YOUR OWN MUSIC
FROM CONCEPT TO INK: AD MEMORIES . A NEW DIGITAL CHALLENGE
A PARTNER IN ADVERTISING . THE LEGEND OF TASCAM SAM

Speaking Musicianese

TASCAM's advertising, sales, and marketing teams in the early days had several unique opportunities. Selling affordable recorders to musicians in the '70s was like promoting water on a desert island, but educating them on the concepts of multitrack recording required a whole new marketing lingo—

musicianese. Most everyone on staff was either an engineer or a musician of good talent, but it took more than just great chops to compress all that knowledge down to a 100-word ad.

"It was a very collaborative, highly productive team approach," recalls Rick Clark, who produced many of the company's ad materials over the years. "We would all sit in the Montebello conference room and put this stuff together with everyone's input, and there was no such thing as a bad idea. We just put it all down and collectively moved towards the strongest position."

Everyone wore a variety of hats on the early '70s core teams, including Dr. Abe, Gary Beckerman, Budd Johnson, David Oren, and Bill Mohrhoff. Johnson wrote the manuals for the original TCA-40 Simul-Sync Series in the late '60s, and helped forge the TASCAM marketing tradition in Montebello, as well. He often collaborated with Dick Rosmini to write promotional copy that would spark 30 years worth of well-crafted marketing messages to follow. One of those gems was the *Home Made With TEAC* instructional album promotion.

Home Made With TEAC *best summed up the company's connection with home recordists. Prophetic liner notes include: "It may be a little early to talk about the historical significance of the multitrack tape recorder, but one thing is for certain—it's here to stay."*

"We would all sit in the Montebello conference room and put this stuff together with everyone's input, and there was no such thing as a bad idea."

Produced by Rosmini, the *Home Made* package included a vinyl LP, and extensive multi-page liner notes to guide musicians through the delicate process of their first multitrack recording experience. Filled with passionate copy and Peter Max-like illustrations, the package centers around how the Hello People spent one summer using a TEAC 3440S to record tracks in Greg Geddes' house that eventually made it to their self-titled, Todd Rundgren-produced album for Warner Brothers. Tips on miking drums, cleaning tape heads, and recording in a kitchen were offered, and the accompanying LP used music tracks produced by Rosmini to demonstrate how best to use the breakthrough A-3340.

"Everyone involved had the feeling that we were participating in a very important, historic era," Johnson recalls of those early TASCAM days. "We knew the technology we were helping musicians to access was affecting the whole industry, and music in general."

Holding novice recordist's hands and encouraging them through the multitracking experience became a TASCAM specialty. Numerous ads, brochures, and in-store promos helped, but engineering products that took into account the novice nature of its users helped even more. Using circuitry that automatically compensated for users unfamiliar with electronics, TEAC and TASCAM gear was often "over-engineered" to record for years without a minute of user maintenance.

"Most users rarely cleaned or calibrated a recorder once it came out of the box," says

David Oren, an original member of TASCAM's early marketing teams. "We were designing for that environment and we wanted the product to meet or exceed the original published specs when a service center finally got ahold of it years later—that was the whole philosophy. God, I still sound like an evangelist!"

Nebraska was one of TASCAM's early promotional opportunities, though one the company didn't care to trumpet too loudly. Bruce Springsteen had recorded the album's tracks on a Model 144 Portastudio in a bedroom, but company engineers and marketers were aware the album's success owed much more to the world's top mastering experts than to the Portastudio—not to mention, of course, the Boss himself. Ardent endorsement hoopla didn't fit the company's philosophy, then or now.

"We didn't want to imply that any Joe could do what Bruce did," says Oren. "For us to say, 'Buy one of these and you, too, will succeed,' would've been ludicrous. We never made a big deal about things like that because it suggested the average individual could do what Springsteen did—without his chops, his skill set, or his mastering engineers. TASCAM never took that kind of an endorsement. There's story after story of big groups using our gear that we could never print. Tons of 80-8 demo tapes were getting dumped to 24-track machines in commercial studios when the energy level just wasn't matching the feel of the home demo, but they just couldn't admit to using affordable gear at home due to their prestige and status."

'From Santa Monica to Montebello'

TASCAM's first sales manager, Budd Johnson, was the only person to have worked both for the original TCA Corporation in Marina Del Rey, and for TASCAM in Montebello. Recognizing early on that simply owning a Martin wouldn't make him the next Bob Dylan, he soon found the thrill of a ground-breaking audio start-up just as intoxicating. "TASCAM was instrumental in helping to change the concept of music as an art form," says Johnson. "It was no longer just a performing art. Bands began to put the bulk of their efforts into producing an album, and then touring to promote it. That was a significant change, and we knew as it was happening that we were all a part of that change."

"...we wanted the product to meet or exceed the original published specs when a service center finally got ahold of it years later—that was the whole philosophy. God, I still sound like an evangelist!"

Roll Your Own Music

Monitor Amplifier
ACCUPHASE
Model P-300

Monitor Speakers (2)
JBL – Model 4315

"A large part of the company philosophy was taught to me by Bill Mohrhoff," says Gregg Hildebrandt. "If we built the right products for a value and told our story, we'd always be successful. Bill really established that kind of thing with the ad agencies a long time ago. It's very easy to get carried away with believing your own press and getting sloppy, which happens to a lot of companies. The bottom line was that if we had to go up against a competitor in a market, then we weren't going to get dragged into playing that type of game."

Taken from a 1976 in-store promotion, the model's "Roll Your Own Music at Home" t-shirt mirrored the grass roots spirit of the times.

HOLDER OF THE WORLD TRACK RECORD.

The 80-8 has become the most popular 8-track multichannel recorder in the world. The results produced on it are a matter of record. Sometimes gold.

To us, pro means results. On demand. For payment. If you agree, see your Tascam Series dealer for the recorders and mixers that prove it.

TASCAM SERIES
TEAC Professional
Products Group

©1979 TEAC Corporation of America, 7733 Telegraph Road, Montebello, CA 90640.

This 1979 ad for the 80-8 focused on the recorder's popularity while subtly addressing the company's "semi-pro" critics—namely, the copy line reading: "To us, pro means results."

From Concept to Ink: Ad Memories

$elling TASCAM products with advertising the past 30 years has generated more than a few interesting

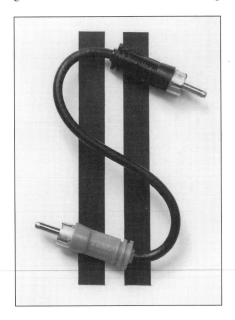

experiences. Truth be told, each ad is a short story in itself that sells a product's best features, helps to educate users on its applications, and offers an inside look at the company behind the imagery, bringing it all to market.

One ad that illustrated the company's resistance against overly aggressive tactics was the TASCAM 58 "antique store" concept from the late '70s. Created at a time when TASCAM's competitors were jumping on the "semi-professional" semantics bandwagon, the ad pictures an ancient camera, a Victrola, and a host of competitors' multitracks in the window of a New York City antique store. The final headline, "TASCAM 58 puts the 1-inch 8-track in its place," though powerful, was a toned-down version of the original copy that read, "Our 50 Series will redefine Otari's dealer network." The marketing team had already grown tired of its

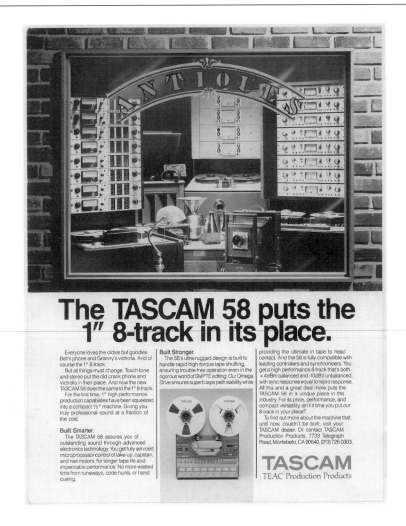

competitors' tactics by that time, yet found the better part of valor in toning down the copy before going to press.

"We had a good laugh with that comp," recalls Rick Clark. "I joked about anonymously faxing it up to somebody at Otari after we changed it, and telling them I had run across it in the TEAC dumpster; but thought better of that and didn't. That comp was one of those ideas you just had to do even though you knew it would never fly. Much to their credit, TASCAM has never been one to do attack advertising."

" 'You've killed my machine!' But it was a great ad that really showed how well-built our equipment was."

This surgically split 40-4 showed off a well-built machine, but was a little bit more than one passionate TEAC engineer could bear.

A stateside ad for the TASCAM Series 40-4 was designed to attract the gaze of gear-loving engineers and electronic fanatics. Halved by a professional metal shop in Montebello, the dissected unit was a wonderful way to show off classic TEAC engineering, but ultimately a painful experience for those who built it in Japan.

"That ad almost got someone fired at TEAC," says Chuck Prada. "When the Japanese build something, there is a feeling for the product that goes far beyond specs. Everybody's working together to build the best of everything, and to see someone take your art and cut it in half is just unacceptable. It's like, 'You've killed my machine!' But it was a great ad that really showed how well-built our equipment was."

PORTASTUDIO.

LEARN ON IT.
REHEARSE ON IT.
CREATE ON IT.

Portastudio gives you all the essential functions of multitrack recording in one compact, self-contained unit.

You can work anywhere you have an electrical outlet. Connect electronic instruments directly. And try out new musical ideas. Will a keyboard work well in the break? Do you want a chorus behind the vocal? With Portastudio, you can find out before you put out hard cash for studio time.

Whether you're recording basic tracks, overdubbing, punching-in or mixing down to another cassette deck, Portastudio helps you get all the signals to the right places.

Portastudio's versatile 4 x 2 mixer section gives you mic/line/tape switching, trim control, high and low EQ, fader, pan and Aux Send for each input. The failsafe group switching matrix lets you record on up to two tracks at the same time. And the master fader gives you overall level control during recording and mixdown.

The full-logic cue system in Portastudio lets you hear everything you're doing all the time. Input and tape cueing, monitoring for recording or mixdown are all available. And every signal can be metered. Coming or going.

TEAC engineers created a totally unique format for Portastudio. Four tracks in sync on cassette tape at 3-3/4 ips. It's fast, simple, reliable and economical.

Portastudio's drive system is built specifically for the rugged needs of multitrack recording. Transport controls are all solenoid-operated for faster, easier switching. And you get a built-in variable speed control that lets you add special effects, fix a flat note or solve timing and cueing problems.

You can work with Portastudio using nothing more than headphones and a microphone. Or send the output through your home audio system. You'll also find the patch points and controls that let you use Portastudio with other equipment like echo units, equalizers and additional mixers.

Nothing else in the world hands you so much multitrack function in such a sensible way. So see your dealer today for a demonstration of the very affordable Portastudio.

TASCAM CREATIVE SERIES
TEAC Professional Products Group

© 1980 TEAC Corporation of America, 7733 Telegraph Road, Montebello, CA 90640. In Canada, TEAC is distributed by White Electronic Development Corporation (1966) Ltd.

One of the first 144 Portastudio ads to spark countless new recording careers, the potent headline copy says it all.

Perhaps no single recording product inspired as much brand loyalty over the years for TASCAM as the 144. Be it for recording demos for multi-platinum albums, or achieving "legend in their own living room" status, the Portastudio instantly became the common denominator for professionals and hobbyists alike. This and many other products created a brand devotion reminiscent of the same loyalty Apple computer users show for their Macs to this day. Like Apple devotees, emerging young musicians and recordists over the past 30 years have seen TASCAM products in every stage of their career and as a result, have developed a powerful brand identification along the way.

One of Rick Clark's first duties when he began doing outsourced ad materials for TASCAM was to learn how to use a Portastudio. Dave Oren handed him an early Model 144, the *Are You Ready For Multitrack?* booklet, a handful of cables, a direct box, and an average mic. He told Clark to keep it as long as he pleased, just so long as he promised to let him hear what he was coming up with. "That was my introduction to multitrack recording," Clark fondly recalls. "It didn't exactly change my career path and turn me into be a rock star, but I never listened to music the same way again. Both as a musician and a music consumer, it changed how I listen to music."

A New Digital Challenge

"My first Portastudio was a life-saver; it really got me on a roll. There was a lot of experimentation on Bowie's *Station To Station*, but all my ideas were gone by the time everyone got into the studio. The Model 144 allowed me to wake up with a little tidbit in my head, and immediately get it down and bring it into the studio. I wrote eight songs in a month on that machine!"

– Carlos Alomar

Songwriter/Musician

(solo, David Bowie, John Lennon)

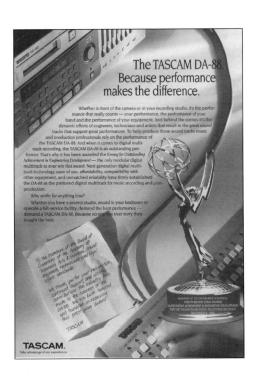

The introduction of the Alesis ADAT in 1991 marked a new era of affordable digital recording—and a new challenge to TASCAM's dominance in the musician recording market. Sales plummeted for any company building reel-to-reel analog recorders when that digital gold rush began, precipitating one of TASCAM's biggest engineering and marketing pushes in company history.

"The ADAT created two opportunities for us," recalls Gregg Hildebrandt. "One was to go after the MI market with our DA-88, the other to go after the professional market. At the same time, we had to decide whether to develop our second generation of 8-bus consoles or to build bigger consoles. By choosing to first go after the high-end market with the DA-88, we allowed competition that we never had before; but going after the more profitable high-end business eventually allowed us to play in the technology areas that were very critical to TASCAM's long-term future. Without the upper end, we never would have formed our current alliances with Timeline, and the MX-2424, MMR-8, or MMP-16 would have never happened. Our music dealers thought we were absolutely insane to walk away from that business, but we couldn't afford to fight both battles at the same time. Eventually, we came back into the MI market with technologies that we've been able to develop ever since, thanks to our success in the high-end market with the DA-88."

Though counter to TASCAM's traditional "hands-off" advertising philosophy, Alesis effectively appealed to the musician's market with simplified comparisons between VHS and Hi-8 technologies. Equating the "bigger is better" logic of analog recording tape to the digital realm was technically misleading, but it spoke directly to the average home recording musician.

"They did a great job of creating the perception that VHS was better simply because it was bigger tape," says Casey Zygmont, who led TASCAM's southern California sales team when the DA-88 launched. "The MI market really went for that because, in their minds, bigger tape was always better: 1/2-inch 8-tracks sounded better than 1/4-inch 8-tracks, 1-inch 16-tracks were better than 1/2-inch 16-tracks, and so on. They even had an ad that said Hi-8 tape is only a 1/4-inch wide and VHS is 1/2-inch, so you get "bigger bits" with the ADAT! You could say that bigger tape is more robust in analog machines, but not with digital."

Zygmont also remembers a brochure and an ad the TASCAM marketing team were preparing that was to answer Alesis' ads directly by comparing the DA-88 to the ADAT. "That brochure would've been slinging mud, and TEAC had never done that type of thing, so we canned it. There was also an ad for the DA-38 at the time that pictured a unit in the middle of the desert and read, 'There's no service station in site, but it doesn't matter because you've got a TASCAM.' That was in direct reference to the early mechanical problems the original ADAT was having back then, though it was a much more subtle message than facing off two totally different technologies."

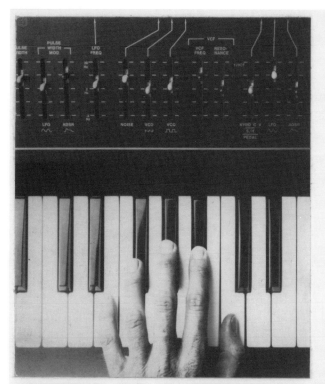

THIS IS WHERE TOMORROW'S GREAT MUSIC IS COMING FROM.

We think musical styles change because musical talents change.

There is hardly a musician making money today who doesn't know as much about recording music as he does about playing it. And recordists know as much about playing music as they do about recording it.

Because both know the equipment that captures music can also be used to improve it.

So while musical styles may change, the interdependence of musician, recordist, and the instruments they use will not. And that is the reason for the TASCAM Series by TEAC.

For not very much money TASCAM lets both musician and recordist get their hands on mixers and recorder/reproducers that let both tailor their music their way.

For every kind of music, for every kind of need, at home and on the road, by price and application, everything we make

has the same goal as everything you make—be the best.

Because it still takes great talent to make great music.

TASCAM SERIES BY TEAC®

A new generation of recording instruments for a new generation of recording artists.

TEAC Corporation of America
7733 Telegraph Road, Montebello, California 90640
In Canada TEAC is distributed by White Electronic Development Corporation (1966) Ltd.

The Model 5-EX shown with four optional 201 input modules. Model 5 shown with optional 204 talk back/slate module.

©TEAC 1977

Two ads that used strong visual messaging to drive home the company's new TASCAM Series by TEAC line in 1977, followed by the 238 Syncaset in 1988.

FINALLY, 8 TRACKS IN THE PALM OF YOUR HAND.

Others have tried. But 8-track capability on a standard audio cassette remained elusive. Until now.

Introducing the remarkable new 238 Syncaset® from Tascam, the company that invented portable, multi-track recording.

If you've been working with a 4-track for pre-production composing or demos, the 238 doubles your capacity right now. Running at 3¾ ips, and taking advantage of Tascam's proprietary head technology, the rack-mountable 238 gives you sound you won't believe was recorded on a standard audio cassette.

But the 238 doesn't stop there. It's fully synchronizable with MIDI/SMPTE time codes, it's got a serial port for computer interfacing and it's designed with open architecture for software upgrades.

Add to that the advantages of full-function remote control, auto punch in/out, shuttling capability and dbx II noise reduction, and you've got a machine that just about does it all.

If this all seems a little too good to be true, talk to your Tascam dealer. To understand how good the 238 Syncaset really is, you'll just have to try your hand at it.

TASCAM

© 1988 TEAC Corporation of America, 7733 Telegraph Road, Montebello, CA 90640. 213/726-0303.

The Legend of TASCAM Sam

Perhaps no single marketing facet of the '70s more symbolized the company's early devotion to the common engineer and musician than the laid-back, cool TASCAM Sam. Reflecting the company's intentions to identify more with the everyday user than erecting a monument to its own greatness, TASCAM Sam was borne of TASCAM's desire to better relate to its end-users, while creating an open channel of customer feedback. Sam has long since been delegated to the company's dusty advertising and marketing bins in the Montebello warehouse, but his legacy lives on every time a customer asks for help, or cares enough to tell TASCAM what they think of its products.

"Nobody outside the company had any idea of who worked for whom," Hildebrandt admits with a grin. "Our goal was to build our image bigger than life, and to not shine the light on the bodies at TEAC. All the dealers wanted to come visit us and see the new plant, but there's never been a

whole lot of things for people to actually see there. We avoided holding dealer meetings in Montebello because we didn't want them to actually see the few people who were building this level of quality product."

"I was the voice of TASCAM Sam when I was there!," laughs Roger Maycock. "Gregg and Bill didn't want to single out any one person within the company. Roland had a Tom Beckman and Otari had a Tim Schaeffer leading those companies, but Sam was our way of creating a figurehead that never existed. He was even listed as the publisher of our *OnSound Magazine,* and became the voice of all things technical for the company. His column was called "Ask TASCAM Sam," where we answered all the Q&A and user tips stuff."

TASCAM Sam created an open conduit of user feedback that the company still enjoys reading today. One can't help but to get a sense of the long-term devotion TASCAM users display when paging through the reams of warranty card statements over the past 25 years in company archives. Every day the phones light up at the company's customer support center. ◉

"ONE, WITH EVERYTHING. TO GO!"

TASCAM Sam says, "Get it while it's hot! Order up a Ministudio™ to go from a participating dealer, and we'll throw in the works: a "Getchagoin' Pack" ($150 value), with everything you need to get started. No extra charges, no hunting for components, and no waiting!"

This is the hot one. Battery-powered and totally self-contained, the Ministudio is flexible, powerful, yet easy to use with professional results using standard audio cassettes.

With all the goodies in your FREE "Getchagoin' Pack," you're ready to record

—right now. Plug in the responsive MC-10 Cardioid mike. Add lightweight HP-308 headphones. A PS-P1 power supply that frees you from battery worries. Studio-proven, alcohol-free TRC recorder care kit. Ten pro-quality, TEAC tapes. A thick stack of TASCAM track sheets. Plus books: "Are you

ready for multitrack?," a handy technical reference and "The MultiTrack Primer," with tips and guidelines from setups and calibration to proper recording techniques.

It's a tasty deal from TASCAM Sam: "Get it quick, and you get it all." But hurry, supplies are limited.

TASCAM
TEAC Professional Division
7733 Telegraph Road, Montebello, CA 90640 • (213) 726-0303

Ministudio is a trademark of TEAC Corporation of America

"A Partner in Advertising"

Rick Clark has been closely associated with TASCAM's marketing teams over the years on some ground-breaking efforts. First with J2 Marketing Services in the early '70s, and then again in 1984 as Rick Clark Advertising, Clark offers a unique, outsourced perspective of TASCAM that's based on years of in-house collaboration with the company since its earliest days.

"Everybody worked within a highly collaborative energy that was taught to me in that environment," says Clark. "That time period laid the groundwork for my love affair with the professional audio industry that still exists today, and impacts my work with companies in completely dissimilar industries. I worked a lot for JBL in those early days, and one of the things I saw in common with both companies was that 80% or better of the key engineering, product development, marketing, and sales personnel were musicians and recordists who were passionate about their art."

WHICH MAGAZINES ARE YOUR BEST SOURCE...

WHAT NEW PRODUCTS WOULD YOU MOST LIKE TO SEE TASCAM MAKE?

STICK D WHAT YOU'RE DOING
AND DO IT BETTER THAN
ANYONE ELSE

This is the part that isn't computerized. Please let us benefit from your comments and be assured that another human being will read them.

ITS OK.
DON'T BE AFRAID!
☺

9101400401

- □ 24 track
- □ 1"C Format
- 62 ☒ 24 or more
- 68 □ 16 or more
- DI PATCHBAY
- 76 □ Sampler
- □ Composer

This is the part that isn't computerized. Please let us benefit from your comments and be assured that another human being will read them.

I am not a sound engineer. I appreciate that
with my limited knowledge, capable competence,
and a machine built with me in mind, I feel
certain that I can professionally record.

3D0009000A

- track 49 □ 24 track
- 57 □ 1"C Format
- 16-20 62 □ 24 or more
- 8 68 □ 16 or more
- □ MIDI PATCHBAY
- encer 76 □ Sampler
- 83 □ Composer

---

human being will read them.

THE DA-88 + 38 JUST AMAZE ME!
MY CLIENTS ARE THRILLED TOO!

5700068103

- □ 24 track
- Format
- 2 ☒ 24 or more
- □ 16 or more
- CHBAY
- □ Sampler
- poser

I am thrilled with the quality of sound from
my Tascam 414. —
  and
I love it's size! The instruction manual
was well presented + easy to understand.
The price was reasonable.
    Thank you!!!
          Bev

9101400401

- 57 □ 1"C Format
- 16-20 62 □ 24 or more
- 7 8 68 □ 16 or more
- □ MIDI PATCHBAY
- uencer 76 □ Sampler
- 83 □ Composer

Great products!
Keep up the good work!

9101400401

- ck 49 □ 24 track
- 57 □ 1"C Format
- 16-20 62 □ 24 or more
- 8 68 □ 16 or more
- MIDI PATCHBAY
- er 76 □ Sampler
- □ Composer

I OWN SO MUCH TASCAM
GEAR, I SHOULD BE A STORE!

5700068103

- 7 □ 1"C Format
- 16-20 62 ☒ 24 or more
- 8 68 □ 16 or more
- MIDI PATCHBAY
- 76 ☒ Sampler
- □ Composer

---

exibility/Function

mendation

aler

This is the part that isn't computerized. Please let us benefit from your comments and be assured that another human being will read them

♡ I LOVE MY ♡
MINISTUDIO!

- 9 □ 24 track
- 1"C Format
- 62 □ 24 or more

This is the part that isn't computerized. Please let us benefit from your comments and be assured that another human being will read them.

I Like TASCAM quality +
and I believe that Tascams
years of experience building
Audio gear results in well thought
out and well made equipment.
  Thank you for doing a great
job,   JBH

9101400401

This is the part that isn't computerized. Please let us benefit from your comments and be assured that another human being will read them.

I LIKE TASCAM TRADE
BECAUSE THEY MAKE GOOD
PRODUCTS.

9101400401

This is the part that isn't computerized. Please let us benefit from your comments and be assured that another human being will read them.

Great Products!

5700068103

This is the part that isn't computerized. Please let us benefit from your comments and be assured that another human being will read them.

Your 424 is just about the coolest thing
ever. Teenage wannabe rock stars everywhere
owe you their souls

9101400401

This is the part that isn't computerized. Please let us benefit from your comments and be assured that another human being will read them.

Please send me more
gear!
Trying to record
need Help!
Use all tascam products

9101400401

BY:

This is the part that isn't computerized. Please let us benefit from your comments and be assured that another human being will read them.

BOUGHT THE TASCAM BECAUSE IT
IS IN EVERY STUDIO I HAVE
BEEN IN.
I LOVE IT.

3D0009000A

This is the part that isn't computerized. Please let us benefit from your comments and be assured that another human being will read them.

I'VE WORKED WITH TASCAM Audio products in the
past and loved the way they hold up as well
As the quality. This is the FIRST TASCAM product
I'M proud to own, and look forward to my next
TASCAM purchase. PLEASE send me some literature
on other TASCAM products. PLEASE continue to
proudly live up to your REPUTATION.
          THANK you

9101400401

Musicians and engineers found the Mr. Natural–like "Tascam Sam" a likable character who encouraged them to offer feedback while learning and using their new recording gear.

WIN A $20,000*

*Approximate value based on manufacturer's suggested prices and TEAC's Nat

The TEAC Tascam Series Studio Giv

sed Values.

Compressor/Limiter
DBX Model 161

Digital Delay
MXR

Graphic Equalizer
UREI Model 530

Line Level Mixer
TEAC Tascam Series—Model 1

Master Recorder
TEAC Tascam Series—Model 25-2

Microphones (6)
TEAC—Model ME-120

Mixing Console
TEAC Tascam Series
Model 10B

Monitor Amplifier
ACCUPHASE
Model P-300

Monitor Speakers (2)
JBL—Model 4315

Patch Bay
TEAC—Model PB64

Recorder/Reproducer
TEAC Tascam Series—Model 80-8

Reverb Unit
AKG—Model BX10

Synthesizer
ARP—Model 2600

Woman
Linda—Model
(shown but not offered)

TEAC
TASCAM SERIES

ay Ends Midnight, November 30, 1976

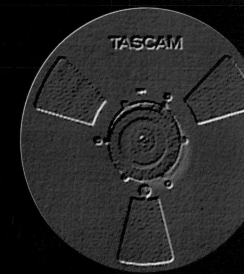

MUSIC & RECORDING TECHNOLOGY 4

WE'RE HERE TO HELP

A HELPING HAND . FACE TO FACE . A MIXER IN EVERY KITCHEN . THE "SEMI-PRO" MISNOMER

A NEW WAY TO HELP . FOUR ESSENTIAL QUALITIES

A Helping Hand

Ask any musician, engineer, or producer what they like most about recording technology, and they'll likely go on about the latest tool allowing them to create their music like never before. Tape hiss is a thing of the past, and today's random-access recordists can cut, copy, and paste an entire arrangement in the time it used to take a 2340 to rewind a 7-inch reel.

better manual, that's usually the *last* place someone looks before ringing up tech support.

Manufacturers of pro and consumer electronics in every sector know the above scenarios intimately, if not even painfully. Educating end-users, dealers, reps, and the market in general about why

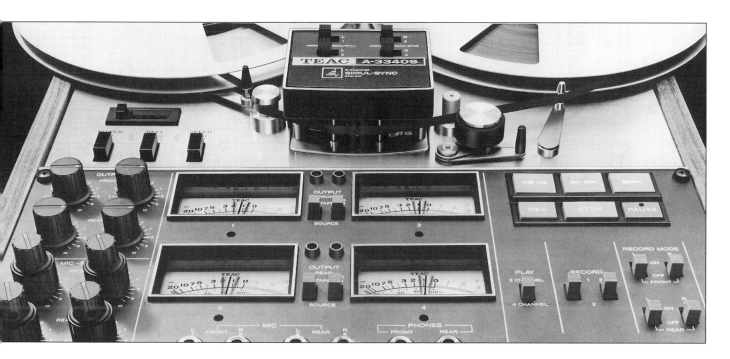

Ask that same person what they like least about new gear, and you'll likely hear a laundry list of complaints about complicated manuals, bottomless menu levels, and holding endlessly for tech support just to grasp the very technology the user is so excited about. Consumers today are more technically savvy and demand even more features, yet their time available for learning new tools and features shrinks every day. Despite manufacturers' best efforts to write a

a new product or technology can change their art is an ongoing process— a process TASCAM has taken a leadership role in over the past 25 years. Hands-on seminars, dealer briefings, trade shows, and Internet newsgroups are just a few ways TASCAM helps users and establishes the company's identity in a constantly changing market.

TASCAM's education challenge in the 1970s was especially extraordinary. A

Hands-on seminars, dealer briefings, trade shows, and Internet newsgroups are just a few ways TASCAM helps users and establishes the company's identity in a constantly changing market.

whole new class of consumers had to be educated on the basics of multitrack recording—basics taken for granted by many of today's recordists and experienced '70s engineers. Convincing musicians that recording technology was no harder to understand than the very instruments they wanted to record was no easy task; assuring them that a new company building products as good as the competition's, for a fraction of the price, proved even more daunting.

"It was critical that engineers and musicians believed we were the Rock of Gibraltar," says Gregg Hildebrandt. "That image was not something that was just haphazardly put together, and we went to great extremes to carry that through. Apple Computer was great with educating users early on and in the past few years, but after Steve Jobs' first tenure, they forgot why people were buying their products to begin with. That's very easy for technology-based companies to do."

Hildebrandt also recalls a similar challenge TASCAM faced with a changing dealer philosophy. "We had to do a significant amount of education because we basically put most of our dealers into the recording business. Very few had sold any recording products prior to TASCAM, so we selected the top music retailers because we knew this was going to be a very time-intensive, one-on-one education process. There was only a certain number of dealers that we could handle at that time."

There are numerous great stories at TASCAM about educating users that illustrate the depth of the company's committment to helping. Regardless of the great effort put into the early education process, everyone at TASCAM quickly learned the virtue of endless patience with end-users.

One such customer in the early '70s purchased an 80-8 and a mixer to record a gospel album. He pressed up the record, and was shocked to learn that the vocals were barely audible in the mix after handing the disc to a local radio station; so he decided to sue TASCAM for $5,000 in damages. Though it may have been cheaper to simply pay him, Bill Mohrhoff knew there was more to it than that, and decided to meet the gentleman in court. Turns out the stereo vocals were recorded with out-of-phase microphones—not a problem during the man's stereo playback at home, but certainly one for a mono broadcast.

Mohrhoff proceeded to educate the court on what phase cancellation was, and that the customer's console had a phase shift switch he didn't use; and the verdict was surprising. The court not only refused the customer's request for cash, but also required him to visit TASCAM, for a week to best learn how to use his new equipment! The end result was a unique teaching opportunity for TASCAM, and one very dedicated, happy customer who couldn't say enough nice things about the company after his week in Montebello.

"Face to Face"

TASCAM's Product Training Manager since 1998, Karl Moet first joined the company as a clinician, trade show coordinator, and product specialist in 1989. An experienced drummer who played on and helped produce Stacey Q's hit, "Two of Hearts", on a TASCAM 85-16, Moet has a friendly and knowledgeable style that's perfect for spreading the TASCAM word. "Gregg hired me to represent end-user needs and to demonstrate how to creatively use TASCAM gear," says Moet, himself a good drummer. "The one subject that I've never grown tired of is Portastudios. Every time I did a clinic, I could see the audience look on in amazement as I performed an overdub. This simple demonstration has always kept the art of recording in a healthy perspective for me."

Moet's two youngest children were fascinated by his 144 Portastudio around the time Wayne's World was released. The kids had a karaoke tape of Queen's "Bohemian Rhapsody" that they played endlessly, and one day recorded it into the 144 when he was at work. "I came home and was amazed to hear all these layers of little munchkin voices singing the song," Moet laughs. "I was floored that my kids figured out how to multitrack all on their own. Needless to say, I included that story in every Portastudio clinic I did from then on."

> "It was critical that engineers and musicians believed we were the Rock of Gibraltar. That image was not something that was just haphazardly put together, and we went to great extremes to carry that through."

A Mixer in Every Kitchen

Another user story from the '70s involved another 80-8. David Oren was working late one night, and answered a phone call from a desperate customer who needed more than just a little hand-holding.

"The guy told me he had just bought an 80-8, but he couldn't get any sound out of it," he recalls. "I asked the guy what else he was using with it, and he said he plugged his microphones directly into the 80-8. I explained that he needed to get ahold of a mixer before he could plug in a mic, to which he replies, 'OK, wait a minute, and I'll go out into the kitchen and get one!' It sounds ludicrous, but's that's where we were with some of these folks! On one side, we had the experienced studio guys who saw the potential in buying TASCAM gear and charging $200 an hour for it, and on the other were guys who didn't know how to plug in a microphone. It was quite a challenge educating users in the early days."

The need to better educate users and dealers today becomes even more crucial as technology advances with every product release. The days when a sales rep with a reasonable handle on the products and a dozen donuts for the music store staff was considered to be doing his job sufficiently are long gone. Dealer and user support seminars escalated in the mid to late '80s, and today's TASCAM events are planned out months in advance for SRO crowds. The brand loyalty and customer devotion to TASCAM products are thanks in large part to these efforts, and have helped the company weather and grow from what would bury any other company without this level of support.

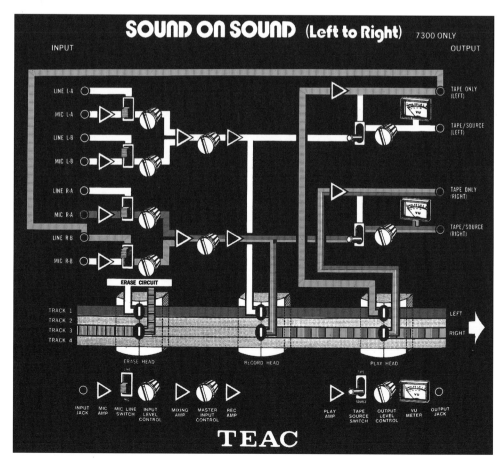

Circa 1966, this signal flow graphic from an instructional counter card was one of TEAC's earliest efforts to help recordists understand the complexities of sound-on-sound recording and playback.

The "Semi-Pro" Misnomer

Oren went on to describe another education and marketing hurdle that proved far tougher than simply directing someone out of the kitchen and into their local music dealer. TASCAM was fulfilling TEAC Japan's best wishes in creating professional audio gear that competed with the industry's top products for a fraction of the cost, and the competition was guardedly nervous about it. Some tried to pigeonhole

TASCAM's products as "semi-professional" and not fitting of the pro studio environment—a position that some users temporarily held at first, as well.

"The people who had money to buy the 80-8 thought it wasn't trustworthy because it didn't cost as much as other multitracks at the time," Oren continues, "and the people who were still trying to afford the 3340 for $1,200 were wondering how they'd ever afford $4,000 for an 8-track. We were caught between a rock and a hard place. We were using unbalanced connectors, and admitted it because it was less expensive, easier to use, and had more headroom. One manufacturer's recorder at the time was being touted as being more professional because it had XLR connectors on it, but it was actually unbalanced on the inside of those connectors, and lost 3 dB on every pass. Games like that were played all the time."

"Most manufacturers recognized the threat that was posed by TASCAM and Fostex, and others that were producing unbalanced products, yet they refused to take us seriously," agrees Hildebrandt. "Meanwhile, we were out there just fulfilling a huge need to customers that those companies were kind of taking for granted. It's amazing how all of a sudden those opinions changed. One of the things we never did was reinforce that we were any less professional than anyone else. In fact, we weren't. We had a musician clientele that was dying to get their hands on our products, but who didn't know what to do with it once they got it; and we also had to deal with issues of dealers that had these clients, but who didn't want to sell recording products. In fact, one of the biggest initial problems was to even get dealers to put our early decks out on

Dealer co-op ads like this one for Leo's Audio in Oakland were in every issue of free local musician mags, such as the legendary BAM (Bay Area Musician).

display because they assumed they were fragile "hi-fi" products the customers might accidentally break. There was frankly nothing we wouldn't do to help the dealers and give them them confidence to make a TASCAM sale, and that we'd stand behind it."

"TASCAM was one of the first to really muster a strong dealer support program," adds Rick Clark. "The materials we developed for them—such as ad slicks for co-op advertising, plenty of collateral materials, and good training—that was all part of a well-managed dealer effort on TASCAM's part."

One such effort was to make it as easy as possible for dealers to create advertisements in the days before desktop publishing allowed anyone to do so. Many early TASCAM dealers were devoted gear gurus but terrible ad copywriters, so Hildebrandt initiated a connect-the-dots dealer program that was practically foolproof. TASCAM's agencies created veloxes of well-written, targeted local ads that would tie into the company's national ad campaign. The national ad goals were to expose the products and create the image for the customer, so TASCAM sent the local ads to the dealers with a space on them that read "Put your store name here." The program worked wonders in local musician magazines like *BAM*, but one unfortunate store missed the instructions, and left a few musicians wondering where the new "Put your store name here" store was in town.

A New Way to Help

TASCAM's leadership role in educating and encouraging buyers and sellers of recording products to make more music continues today. A new webmaster was hired in 2000 to integrate numerous bulletin board groups that cater specifically to everything from Portastudio users, to post-production pros; and no less than seven new product specialists have come aboard since 1998 to expand the company's focus and sphere of expertise. Each specialist is responsible for monitoring and responding to user newsgroup requests on a daily basis to harvest invaluable customer feedback and to keep in touch.

"When you hear about manual problems enough times, it goes right to the top of the list," says Gene Joly, TEAC's V.P. of Operations. "We're now sourcing more manuals, and putting a lot of effort into making them the best they can be. We also regularly get proposed to not include a printed manual in the box and just include a CD-ROM, or simply point people to our website. It's cheaper for us that way, but not for the end user who has to log on and wait to download a PDF file." ●

"Four Essential Qualities"

"Anyone providing customer support needs to possess the qualities of four different people," says Neal Faison, TEAC/TASCAM's Operation Support Manager since 1986, who often goes from helping an audio pro and first-time VCR user from one call to the next. "You need the deductive reasoning of a Sherlock Holmes to find out what's really wrong, especially if they're upset; the technical chops of a Ken Pohlmann to understand the product and what it's capable of doing; the neutral, diplomatic skills of a Henry Kissinger, especially if the customer is upset with a dealer or service center; and finally, the patience and demeanor of Mahatma Ghandi to deal with everyone at once. Each call requires a bit of each of these trademarks. If you have all four of these qualities, you can help anyone."

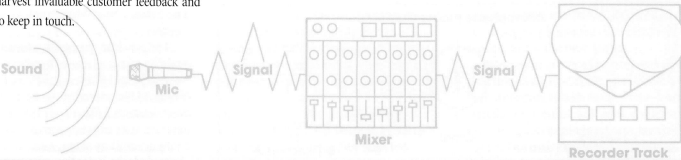

Sound
Mic
Signal
Mixer
Signal
Recorder Track

"When you hear about manual problems enough times, it goes right to the top of the list."

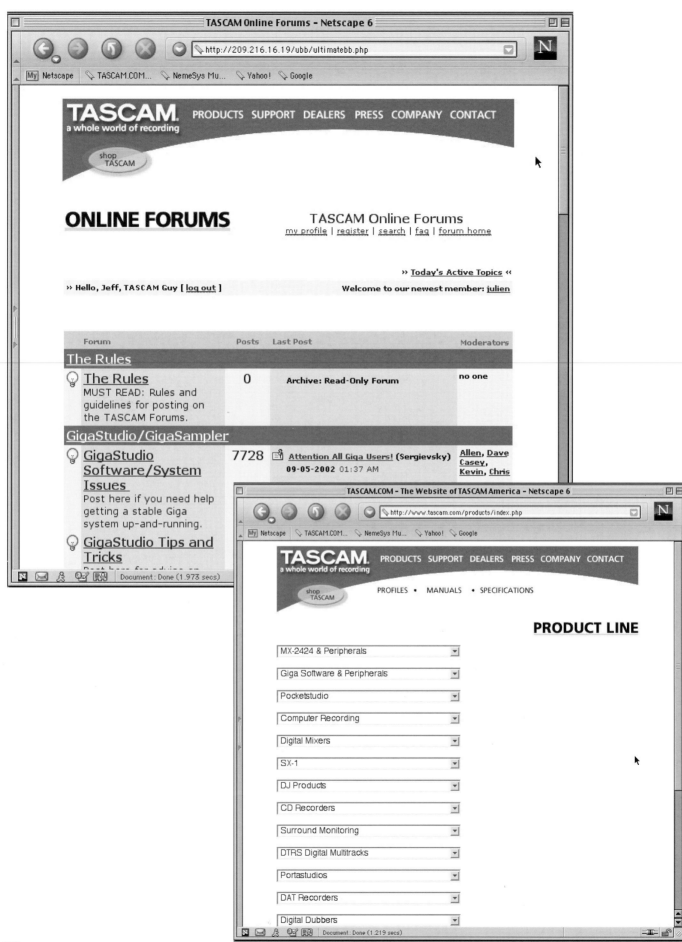

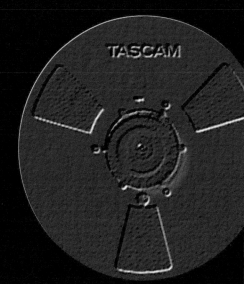

STAFF STORIES AND 5
PROTOTYPE DELIGHTS

CLASSIC YARNS. TUBES, SMOKE, AND MIRRORS . PROTOTYPE DELIGHTS

The voice of R2D2, and all special dialogue and sound effects, were recorded and mixed on **TEAC** and **TASCAM SERIES** equipment...

STAR WARS

Classic Yarns

Digging through three decades of TASCAM technology unearthed a wealth of funny, insightful stories along the way. Tales of flamingo legs, space shuttles, kitchen mixers, court cases, dissected multitracks, and Sambo's placemats dot the preceding chapters in illuminating 25 years of evolutionary product development. But wait, there's always more! Fifteen interviews with past and current alumni; a dozen sound bites from the likes of Diddley, Keltner, Duke, and Frampton; and archaelogical journeys in the company's Montebello warehouse have netted enough stories to fill five books with TASCAM lore alone.

equipment..." was a powerful message, but two things happened to prematurely end the promotion: the *Star Wars* phenomenon caused most of the R2D2s to be stolen by adoring fans within the first week of the movie's release, and budget adjustments axed the promotional tape package and a planned national ad campaign before anyone else knew about TASCAM's role in the movie.

"It was amazing that we even got the rights to distribute the soundtrack for such a major movie," recalls David Oren, a big part of that effort. "We were so helpful to them that they actually allowed us to

> ## "It was amazing that we even got the rights to distribute the soundtrack for such a major movie."

R2D2 Used an 80-8

Few are aware of one of the classiest promotions to ever grace the audio industry. Bill Callfield befriended Ben Burt, the latter at the time using TASCAM gear in his Boston basement to record all the voice and sound effects for the R2D2 character in the first *Star Wars* movie. Burt arranged a promotion deal between TASCAM and George Lucas to put the John Williams score on one tape reel and the R2D2 effects on another, wrap an expensive booklet and package around both reels, and give it to a very select group of producers, studios, dealers, and record labels when the movie hit.

The R2D2 promo was an actual size, cut-out version of the likable robot that was up in every theater lobby screening the movie. *"The voice of R2D2, and all special dialogue and sound effects, were recorded and mixed on TEAC and TASCAM Series*

give away the original soundtrack on a 7-inch reel of tape! I think budgets just got tight, but it also got shot down because management thought *Star Wars* might be a kid's movie—a fantasy that TASCAM shouldn't be associated with. Those tapes were never distributed."

A Real Pioneer

Owing to his background in electronic engineering, selling TASCAM gear at West L.A. Music was Gregg Hildebrandt's favorite pastime. His first big sale was to Walter Becker of Steely Dan, who needed an extra set of eyes, hands, and ears in setting up his new Model 10 mixer and Series 70 8-track recorder at one of the first affordable home studios in Los Angeles—or anywhere, for that matter.

"Neither one of us knew or had any idea how to use it," laughs Hildebrandt of Becker's TASCAM installation.

Operations manuals, like this one for the 80-8 recorder, helped countless engineers and musicians tame a new learning curve.

"I delivered it to his house, and we spent two continuous days unpacking the gear, hooking it up, reading the manuals, and trying to adjust the calibrations and such. We had a great time with it. Steely Dan was at their peak at that time, and Becker really was one of the pioneers of the whole home studio revolution."

The Pope and the Lincoln Tunnel

An AES show in New York once corresponded with a visit from the Pope. To make matters worse, the hotel where TASCAM was holding a meeting was directly in line with the masses, and Karl Moet had a van full of company gear he was bent on delivering. With the van jam-packed, there were no seats for the two techs joining him for the cross-papal journey, and there wasn't a cab for miles.

"The techs squeezed in between the gear," laughs Moet, "and it looked like one of those college pranks in a VW Bug. As luck would have it, I take off just ahead of the visiting Pope's motorcade, thinking I can beat them into the city. I make it as far as the Lincoln Tunnel, and the traffic just stops. I felt so bad for those guys trapped in the back, wedged between all the gear, because we sat in that tunnel for a long time."

"Tubes, Smoke, and Mirrors"

Before being hired as TASCAM's Los Angeles area sales rep in 1991, Casey Zygmont worked at Guitar Center in San Francisco in the '70s, and spent seven years with an audio rep firm called Just Noticeable Difference. He also owned a demo studio in the Mission neighborhood, and one night at GC, he bumped into a few members of the Tubes, whom he had done some work for in those days (remember Quay Lewd?). "I actually got in a little trouble with them once," laughs Zygmont. "A couple of them were in the store buying gear one night, and we ended up dragging all this TASCAM stuff into the acoustic guitar room to set up a makeshift studio. We were there until two or three in the morning, and the next day I get called into the boss's office. He says, 'I got a call that says you logged out with the alarm company at 3 A.M. What were you doing at three in the morning here!?' When I told him, he said 'Oh, well, that's OK.'"

Zygmont recalls the first DA-88 prototype, shown at AES in San Francisco in a locked room. "We were in a tight spot when the ADAT was announced because we didn't have our machine on the immediate horizon," he continues. "That prototype was simply a black box with light bulbs inside of it to light the front panel. It had eight meters on the front and a fake transport door, but on the back there was absolutely nothing except an AC cord for the light bulbs! We had this velvet shroud over it that we would dramatically pull off to unveil the DA-88 when dealers came in to see it. It was a smoke and mirrors game because we needed everyone to see we had something on the way."

Prototype Delights

This particular TASCAM 44 was definitely not the prototype version rescued from a pawn shop or dropped down the stairs.

"This was a hand-built machine," Chuck Prada recalls. "When you compare it to production models, you can tell because there's too many wires. Well, this one eventually broke down, and the guy took it to a local service center. They told him it was a prototype, and could also tell he wasn't the one who stole it."

Parts Were Scattered Everywhere

Another Summer NAMM was the site of the TM-D1000's debut. TASCAM had a few prototypes for display that needed some work before hitting the trade show floor, so each was disassembled in a hotel room. Parts were left strewn about the room when the techs broke for dinner, but after the previous day's long flight, the room looked like a tornado on their return. The mixers performed flawlessly, despite the techs never figuring out what to do with a number of leftover parts that they couldn't seem to fit into the puzzle.

Karl Moet tells a similar story about the first trade show he managed for TASCAM. Things were going swimingly until the pre-show sales meeting ended, and he returned to work late into the night on the booth.

"I had moved gear from the show floor to Anaheim Hilton," Moet recalls, "and when I returned to the floor, I noticed a visiting tech from Japan—who did not speak English—was disassembling an ATR-60/16, and had it spread out all over the exhibit. I knew he understood why I was upset, and he started to hurriedly put the deck back together. When I asked him why he took it apart in the first place, he explained through an interpreter that he never gets a chance to do things like this

Every manufacturing company faces the same dilemma described by Zygmont. Time-to-market is crucial to a product's and company's success; and it's especially unforgiving when preparing prototypes for pivotal trade shows and making last-second adjustments. Good and bad beta versions are both of interest to the true gear head when looking back, even if one in particular had a brush with the law.

You Have the Right to an Attorney

The original prototype for the TASCAM Model 44 recorder was a rugged machine. The production versions could roll down a flight of stairs and still catch the next punch-in on the downbeat, but this beta met a different fate. It was stolen somewhere between the truck and the McCormick Center at a Summer NAMM show, and eventually sold to an innocent audio bystander. Picture someone selling a hot proto-44 out of a van, cables included.

"I used that same unit in my studio for years— damaged heat sync and all. TASCAM builds tanks!"

back in Tokyo, because there's just not enough room. He saw all this open space in the booth, and wanted to get into the ATR, which was quite understandable."

Codename: Elephant

The TMD-8000's interface was an awesome thing of beauty and TASCAM's first digital mixer. Given the privilege of code-naming all in-house R&D projects, TEAC's engineers had annointed the 8000 as "Elephant"; and at the same time were working on "Bear": the TMD-4000's prototype. TASCAM was giving away a Porta 03 to the one Full Sail Recording student who came up with the best name for the then-unnamed TMD-8000, but despite lots of great ideas, nothing stuck. Montebello and Tokyo didn't want another numerical name, but couldn't come up with anything themselves before the show; so they named it the TMD-8000, and carried on with preparing the prototype as such.

"The sample we received just days before the show said 'Elephant' right where the model number was supposed to be— silkscreened right on the chassis itself!," laughs Gregg Hildebrandt. "Bill Mohrhoff and I took one look at it and said, 'Oh, my God, we can't do that because it'll be called the Elephant for eternity if we introduce it like that.' We ran all over Los Angeles, trying to match the exact gray paint with a PMS swatch to come up a temporary logo that would cover the name. Tokyo said they had been working with the sample for so long that they forgot they had ever put the nickname on it."

It Takes a Lickin'

As mentioned earlier, the first three DA-88 prototypes in the country were furiously shuttled all over the country for rep and dealer clinics. The prototype flight cases were checked in as luggage, and handed off between fifty airline connecting flights that included a stop at Denver's old Stapleton Airport.

"I was waiting at the carousel when a big, blue flight case came tumbling down the treadmill," remarks Karl Moet. "This 70-pound case just crashes into the rubber bumpers real hard, and upon opening it, I saw that the heat sync on the back panel of the DA-88 was completely pushed back into the frame! When I arrived at the dealer that night, there was a line of customers waiting in the driving snow to see the DA-88. After warming it up, I plugged the DA-88 in and discovered that it not only lit up, but it actually played the demo tape and was completely functional—just amazing. I used that same unit in my studio for years— damaged heat sync and all. TASCAM builds tanks!" ●

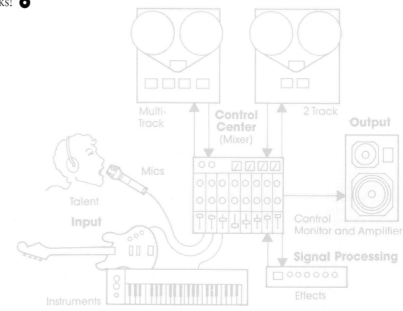

APPENDICES 6

SCHEMATICS . SPECIFICATION SHEETS . EARLY PRICE SHEETS

Appendices: Schematics

Model 144 Block Diagram

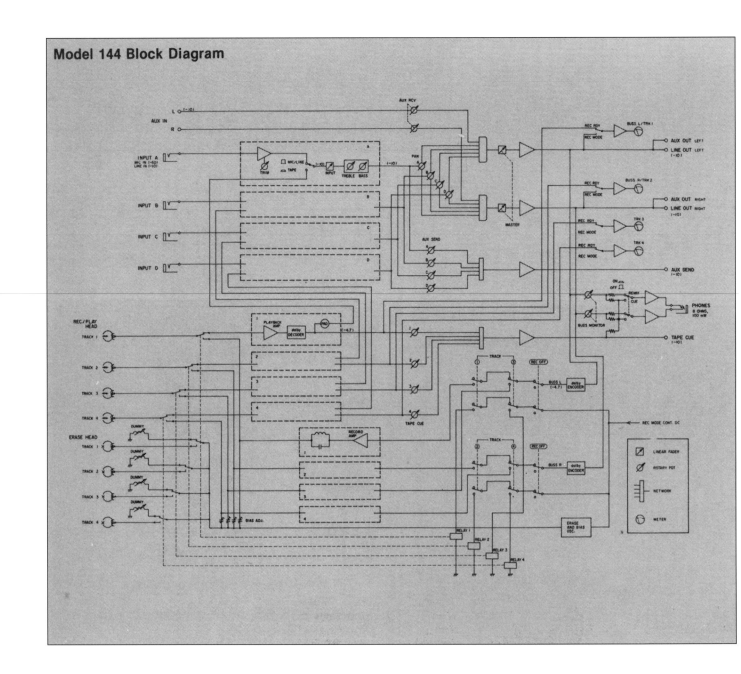

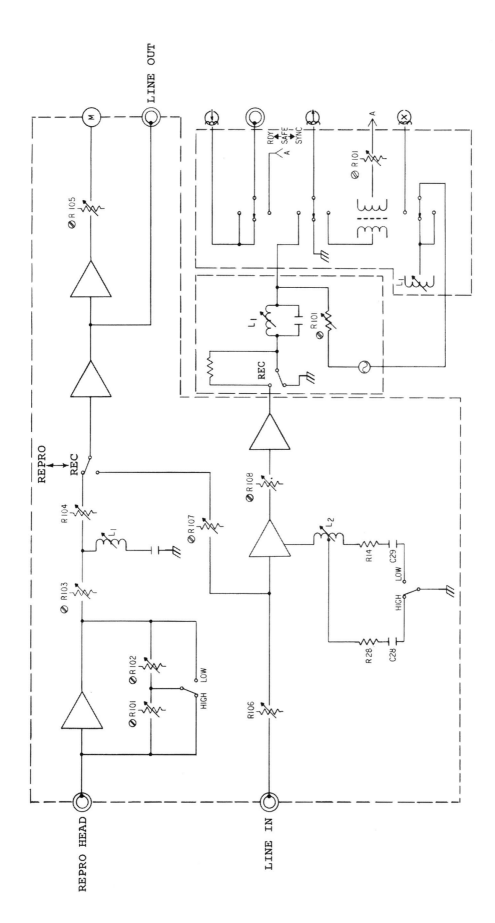

701 ELECTRONICS SIMPLIFIED SCHEMATIC

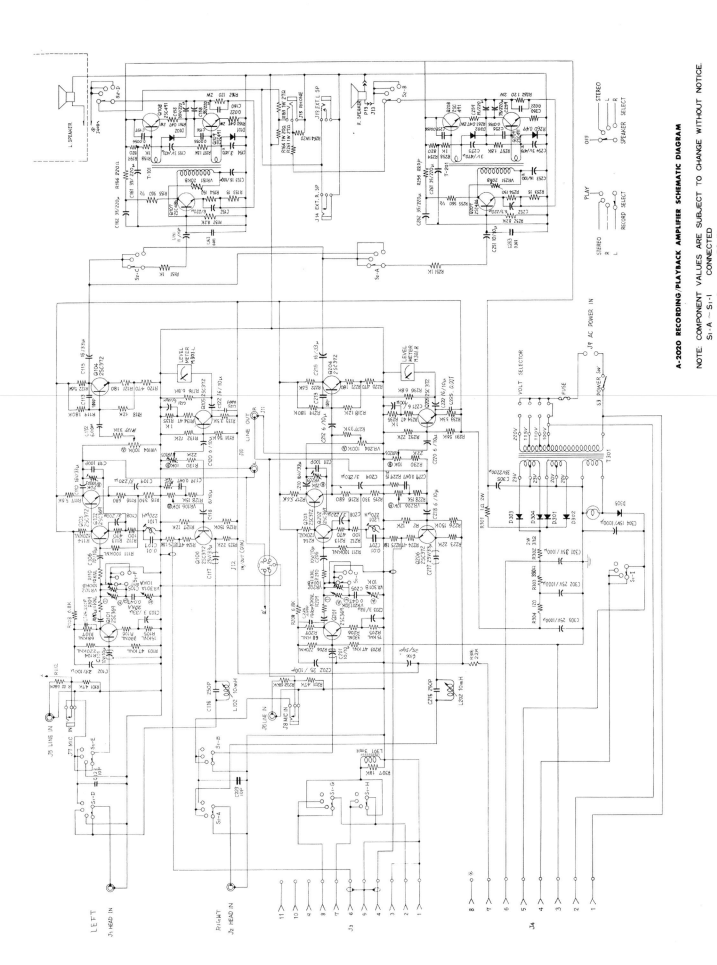

A-2020 RECORDING/PLAYBACK AMPLIFIER SCHEMATIC DIAGRAM

NOTE: COMPONENT VALUES ARE SUBJECT TO CHANGE WITHOUT NOTICE.

S1-A ~ S1-1

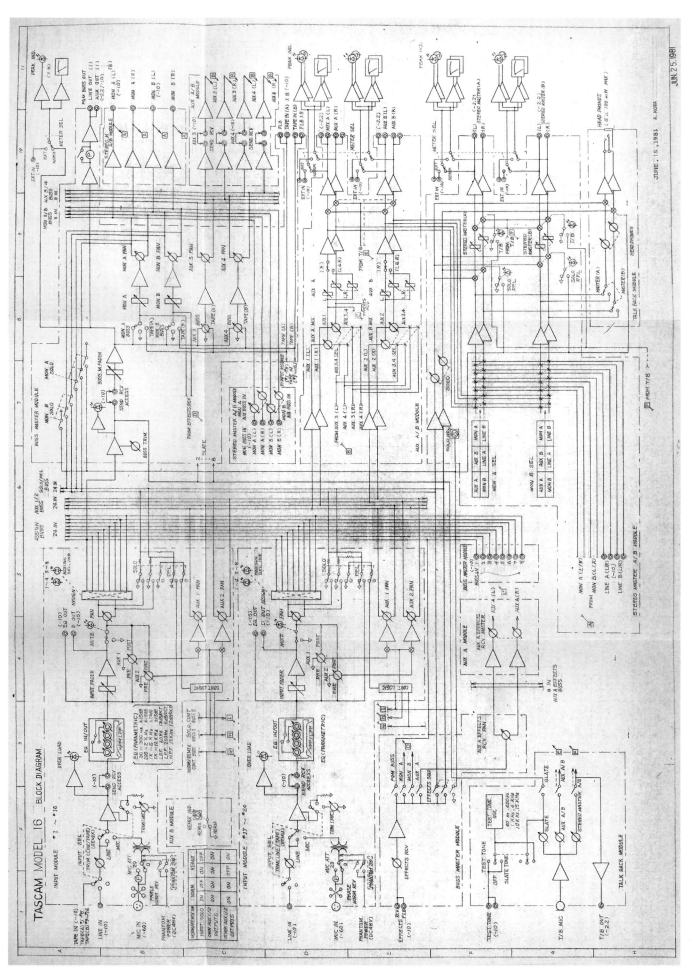

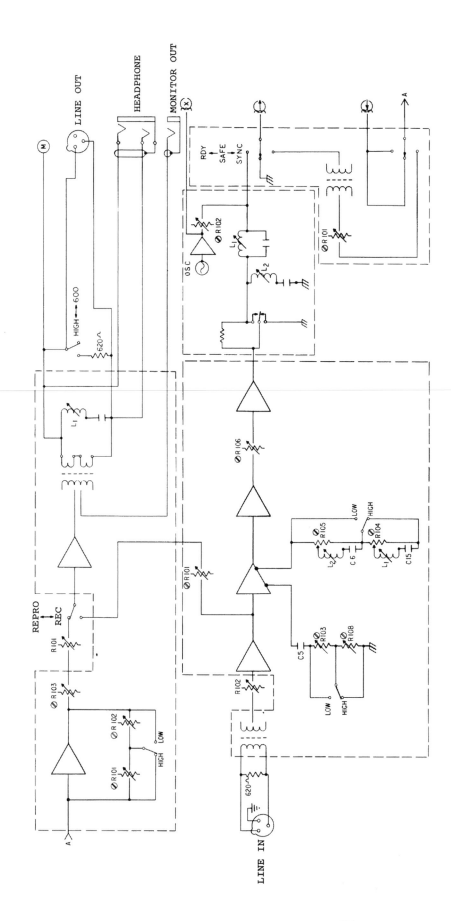

501 ELECTRONICS SIMPLIFIED SCHEMATIC

Block diagram

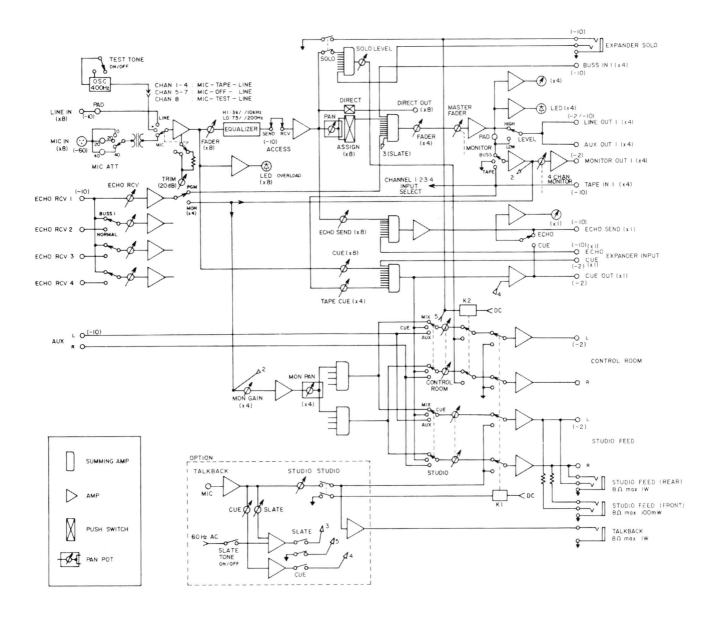

Specification Sheets

SERIES 70 SPECIFICATIONS
All Series 70 specifications based on use of 3M #206 tape

FREQUENCY RESPONSE: Reproduce & Overall	40 Hz-18 kHz ±2 dB at 15 ips 40 Hz-15 kHz ±2 dB at 7½ ips	
SIGNAL-TO-NOISE RATIO, Overall (Referenced to peak record level)	Full Track: Half Track:	greater than 65 dB, WTD greater than 56 dB, UNWTD greater than 63 dB, WTD greater than 54 dB, UNWTD
INSTANTANEOUS SPEED VARIATION: (Measured with calibrated flutter tape)	0.05% WTD RMS (NAB) at 15 ips 0.07% WTD PEAK (ANSI) at 15 ips 0.08% WTD RMS (NAB) at 7½ ips 0.15% WTD PEAK (ANSI) at 7½ ips	
CROSSTALK:	Overall: 50 dB at 1 kHz channel to channel 48 dB at 100 Hz	
DISTORTION: Record and Reproduce (without tape)	Less than 0.5% THD at +10 VU	
SPEED ACCURACY: (through 3600 feet)	99.5%	
EQUALIZATION:	NAB	
ERASURE: (400 Hz at +10 VU reference)	Greater than 65 dB	
RECORD LEVEL CALIBRATION:	Referenced to 185 nWb/m	

	501 ELECTRONICS	701 ELECTRONICS
INPUT IMPEDANCE:	Mic: Nominal 200 Ohms, balanced or unbalanced Line: 600 Ohms, balanced or unbalanced	Mic: None Line: 50K Ohms, unbalanced
LINE OUTPUT LEVEL:	+4 dBm (adjustable)	Nominal .3 V RMS (−10 dB), unbalanced; into 10K Ohms or higher
HEADRROOM (without tape):	20 dB over rated output level	
HEADPHONE OUTPUTS:	3-circuit jack, 600 Ohms, balanced	None
POWER REQUIREMENTS:	117 V AC; 60 Hz; nominal 200 W	

Model 5
Specifications

1. 8-in/4-out

2. Input selector
Chan 1-4 Mic/Tape/Line
Chan 5-7 Mic/Off/Line
Chan 8   Mic/Test/Line

3. Mic input
1) Nominal impedance — 200 ohms
2) Nominal input level — −50dB (0dB = 1V)
3) Minimum input level — −72dB (0dB = 1V)
4) Maximum input level — +25dB (0dB = 1V)

4. Line input
1) Line impedance — Greater than 50K ohms
2) Nominal input level — −10dB (0.3V)
3) Minimum input level — −26dB (50mV)
4) Maximum input level — +30dB (30V)

5. Line output/Aux. output
1) Load impedance — Greater than 10K ohms
2) Nominal output level — −10dB (0.3V), −2dB (0.78V) (switchable)
3) Maximum output level — +18dB (7.8V)

6. 4 channel monitor output
1) Load impedance — Greater than 10K ohms
2) Nominal output level — −2dB (0.78V)
3) Maximum output level — +18dB (7.8V)

7. 2 channel monitor output (for control room and studio)
1) Load impedance — Greater than 10K ohms
2) Nominal output level — −2dB (0.78V)
3) Maximum output level — +18dB (7.8V)

8. Frequency response — 30Hz −20KHz, ±2dB

9. Equivalent input noise — 125dB

10. Signal to noise ratio, overall (measured at nominal input levels)
1) One input (mic or line) — Greater than 75dB WTD 70dB UNWTD
2) 8 inputs (mic or line) — Greater than 65dB WTD 60dB UNWTD

11. Equalization — Peak and dip type, ±15dB continuously variable
Hi band — 3KHz-10KHz switchable
Lo band — 75Hz-200Hz switchable

12. Crosstalk — Greater than 60dB (at 1KHz)

13. Distortion overall
(mic input to output) — 0.3% THD maximum

14. Fader attenuation — Greater than 60dB

15. Send and receive data
1) Accessory send level — Nominal −10dB (0.3V) into 10K ohms or higher
2) Accessory receive level — Nominal −10dB (0.3V) into 10K ohms or higher
3) Echo send level — Nominal −10dB (0.3V) into 10K ohms or higher
4) Echo receive level — Nominal −10dB (0.3V) into 10K ohms or higher

16. Auxiliary input, Bus input, Tape input
1) Input impedance — Greater than 10K ohms
2) Nominal level — −10dB (0.3V)

17. Solo input (for Expander Module)
1) Input impedance — Greater than 10K ohms
2) Nominal level — −10dB (0.3V)

18. Echo input (for Expander Module)
1) Input impedance — Greater than 10K ohms
2) Nominal level — −10dB (0.3V)

19. Cue input (for Expander Module)
1) Input impedance — Greater than 10K ohms
2) Nominal level — −2dB (0.78V)

20. Cue output
1) Load impedance — Greater than 10K ohms
2) Nominal level — −2dB (0.78V)

21. Direct output
1) Load impedance — Greater than 10K ohms
2) Nominal level — −10dB (0.3V)

22. Headphone
1) Load impedance — Greater than 8 ohms
2) Maximum output — Front: 100mW
Rear: 1 Watt (2.8V)

23. Power requirements — 117V AC, 50/60Hz, 40W

24. Dimensions (WHD)
23⅛, 7½, 24½

25. Weight
62 lbs.

A-2340SX Specifications

Tape format	quarter-inch, 4 tracks
Reel size	7'' and 5''
Tape speed	7¹/₂ ips and 3³/₄ ips
Line input	100 mV
	Impedance. 50 k ohms,
	unbalanced
Line output	0.3 V
	Load impedance: greater than
	10 k ohms, unbalanced
Equalization	NAB standard
Speed accuracy	±0.5%
Wow and flutter	0.08% RMS(NAB), weighted at 7¹/₂ ips
	0.10% RMS(NAB), weighted at 3³/₄ ips
	Measured with flutter test tape
Overall frequency	
response	40 Hz—18 kHz, ±3 dB at 7¹/₂ ips
	40 Hz—10 kHz, ±3 dB at 3³/₄ ips
Signal to noise	55dB weighted. referenced to
	3% T.H.D. level
T.H.D. overall	1% at normal operating level
Crosstalk	greater than 50 dB at 1 kHz
Power req.	100/117/220/240 V AC.
	50/60 Hz. 110 W
Dimensions	440 x 475 x 220 mm
(W x H x D)	[17¹/₄'' x 18³/₄'' x 8³/₄'']
Weight	21 kg [48 lbs. 4 oz.] net

Improvements may result in changes of features or specifications without notice.

Model 80-8 Specifications

Tape format	half-inch, 8 tracks
Reel size	10¹/₂''
Tape speed	15 ips
Line input	−10 dB (0.3 V)
	Impedance: greater than 20 k ohms,
	unbalanced
Line output	−10 dB (0.3 V)
	load impedance. greater than
	10 k ohms, unbalanced
Record level	0 VU referenced to 3 dB above
calibration	185 nWb/m of tape flux. adjustable
Equalization	IEC standard
Speed accuracy	±0.5%
Wow and flutter	0.04% RMS(NAB), weighted
	0.06% peak(ANSI), weighted
	Measured with flutter test tape.
Starting time	less than 0.5 sec.
Overall frequency	40 Hz—18 kHz, ±3 dB
response, sync mode	
Signal to noise	65 dB weighted, 60 dB unweighted.
	referenced to 3% T.H.D. level (10 dB
	above 0 VU) at 400 Hz
Distortion	1% at 400 Hz, 0 VU
T.H.D. overall	3% at 10 dB above 0 VU
Crosstalk	greater than 45 dB of 400 Hz
Erasure	greater than 65 dB at 1 kHz,
	+ 10 VU reference
Power req.	100/117/220/240 V AC.
	50/60 Hz 200 W
Dimensions	445 x 535 x 305 mm
(W x H x D)	[17¹/₂'' x 21'' x 12'']
Weight	35 kg [77 lbs.] net

Improvements may result in changes of features or specifications without notice.
"dbx" is a trademark of dbx Incorporated.

The 85-16 is available in four types—A, B, C, and D—according to dbx system, line input/output level and impedance, described in the chart below.

	dbx	In/Out level, imp.
85-16A	×	−10 dBv/−10 dBv, 50 k ohms UNBAL.
85-16B	○	−10 dBv/−10 dBv, 50 k ohms UNBAL.
85-16C	×	+4 dBv/+4 dBv, 600 ohms BAL.
85-16D	○	+4 dBv/+4 dBv, 600 ohms BAL.

Model 85-16 Specifications

Tape format	16 tracks, 1-inch tape width
Reel size	10¹/₂'' maximum, NAB (large) hub only
Tape speed	15 inches per second; Variable,
	±10% relative to 15 ips
Speed accuracy	±0.3%
Starting time	Within 1 second for rated speed and
	3 seconds to reach RMS flutter of
	less than 0.05%
Wow and flutter	0.03% RMS weighted (NAB); ±0.04%
	peak weighted (ANSI): (measured with
	flutter test tape)
Overall frequency	40 Hz—18,000 Hz ±3 dB (Sync and
response	Repro mode)
Total harmonic	
distortion (THD)	1% at 0 VU; 1,000 Hz
Record electronics	
headroom	28 dB or greater above nominal level
	at 1,000 Hz
Signal-to-noise	67 dB weighted or 62 dB unweighted
	with dbx noise reduction bypassed.
	87 dB weighted with dbx noise
	reduction.
Crosstalk (any	Better than 45 dB down @ 1,000 Hz
adjacent tracks)	
Erasure depth	75 dB or greater at 1,000 Hz
Input	
Level	−10 dB (0.3 V) nominal
Impedance	50 k ohms; unbalanced
Line output	
level	−10 dB (0.3 V) nominal;
	+18 dB (8.0 V) max.
Impedance	Greater than 10 k ohms; unbalanced
Connectors	RCA jacks for all inputs and outputs
Indicators	16 illuminated VU meters
Record Level	
Calbration	0 VU referenced to 250 nWb/m (nano
	Webers per meter) tape flux level
Equalization	IEC standard
Bias and erase	
frequency	150,000 Hz.
Motors	2 DC servo-controlled reel motors;
	direct-drive DC Servo Capstan motor
Power mains	100/117/220/240 V AC,
	50/60 Hz, 350 W
Dimensions (W x H x D)	
Assembled Unit	615 x 1,090 x 550 mm
	[24¹/₄'' x 43'' x 21⁵/₈'']
Weight	95 kg [209 lbs.] net

Improvements may result in changes of features or specifications without notice.
"dbx" is a trademark of dbx Incorporated.

Model 144 Specifications

Mic/Line Input (x4)
Mic or line Impedance	10 k ohms or less
Input impedance	60 k ohms
Nominal Input Level	Mic −60 dBv (1 mV);
	Line −10 dBv (0.3 V)
Minimum Input Level	−66 dBv (0.5 mV)
Maximum Input Level	+8 dBv (2.5 V)

Aux Input (x2)
Input Impedance	65 k ohms
Nominal Input Level	−10 dBv (0.3 V)

Line Output (x2), Aux Out (x2)
Output Impedance	200 ohms
Load Impedance	10 k ohms or higher
Nominal Output Level	−10 dBv (0.3 V)
Maximum Output	
Level	+15 dBv (5.6 V)

Headphone Output (Stereo)
Load Impedance	8 ohms or higher
Maximum Output	100 mW @ 8 ohms

Tone Controls
Treble	Variable ±10 dB @ 10 kHz
Bass	Variable ±10 dB @ 100 Hz
Recording Tape	Compact cassette, C-30/60/90—use
	a cobalt or CrO₂ tape that requires
	high-bias level (chrome position) and
	70-microsecond EQ (TDK-SA MAXELL
	UDXL-II, or equivalent)
Record Tracks	4-track, one direction (Special format)
Record Channels	
(Electronics)	2 with full-time Dolby* encoding
	(switchable to the 4 record tracks)
Playback Channels	4 with full-time Dolby* decoding
Normal Tape Speed	3³/₄ ips ±1%
Pitch Control (VSO)	±15% of normal tape speed
Recording Time	15 minutes for C-60

Heads	4-channel erase (ferrite/permalloy);
	4-channel record/playback (permalloy)
Motors	1 FG servo-controlled DC capstan
	motor and 1 DC reel motor
Wow & Flutter	±0.06% max. weighted: 0.04% RMS,
	weighted (measured with flutter test
	tape)
Fast Wind Time	70 seconds for C-60

Frequency Response
Mixer Section	20 Hz—20,000 Hz
Recorder Section	20 Hz—18,000 Hz (40 Hz—12,500 Hz
	±3 dB @ 0 VU)

Total Harmonic Distortion
Mixer Section	0.3% @ 1,000 Hz, nominal level
Recorder Section	2% @ 315 Hz, 0 VU (overall)

Signal-to-Noise Ratio
Mixer Section	68 dB weighted, mic in to line out
	(any channel)
Recorder Section	63 dB, weighted (ref. to 315 Hz,
	250 nanowebers per meter)

Crosstalk
Mixer Section	65 dB @ 1,000 Hz
Recorder Section	50 dB @ 1,000 Hz
Erasure	65 dB @ 1,000 Hz
Power Requirements	100/117/220/240 V AC, 50/60 Hz
	117 V AC, 60 Hz (U.S.A. CANADA)

Dimensions
(W x H x D)	460 x 120 x 370 mm
	[18¹/₈'' x 4³/₄'' x 14⁵/₈'']
Weight	9 kg [20 lbs.] net

TASCAM MODEL DA 50

MAIN FEATURES

- 4 ZD circuits (L/R, record (A/D), playback (D/A), independent).
- Twin ADC's with 10 Bit Dither.
- Twin DAC's with 12 Bit Dither.
- Oversampling digital filter.
- Direct-coupled linear phase circuit.
- Tape transport by 4-DD motors (for drum x 1, capstan x 1, reel x 2).
- Mono-crystal silver-coating cable for internal wiring.
- Separate power supply transformer for digital and analog section.
- Glass epoxy PCB's.
- Slot-in type tape loading mechanism by infrared tape sensor.
- 25-segment peak level meters with variable peak hold time control (0-2 sec).
- Built-in AC line noise filter.
- Brightness switchable (NORMAL/DIM) FL display.
- Intelligent desk-top type hard-wired remote control unit.
- Rack Mount.
- Individual Internally Shielded Chassis for Power Supply, Mechanism, Digital, Analog, Control, and Servo Circuits.
- Power Supplies using Independent Transformers for Digital and Analog Circuits.

MAIN FUNCTIONS

- Blank search
- Renumber function
- Auto rec mute
- Counter mode: Index/Remain time/Absolute time/Program time

- Direct search
- Cue/review
- Music skip
- 2-way repeat: All/A-B
- Start ID/Skip ID

- Inputs:
  - Analog Balanced (L/R, XLR type)
  - Unbalanced (L/R, RCA pin)
  - Digital Digital Audio Interface format
    - Optical x 1
    - Coaxial x 1
- Outputs:
  - Analog Balanced (L/R, XLR type)
  - Unbalanced (L/R, RCA pin)
  - Digital Digital Audio Interface format
    - Optical x 1
    - Coaxial x 1

MAIN SPECIFICATIONS (PROVISIONAL)

• Tape Speed:	8.15 mm/sec
• Sampling Frequency:	48 kHz (Rec/Play)
	44.1 kHz (Play)
	32 kHz (Digital in; Rec/Play)
• Signal-to-Noise Ratio:	better than 92 dB
• Total Harmonic Distortion:	less than 0.005% (1 kHz)
• Total Frequency Response:	1 Hz − 22 kHz ± 0.5 dB
• Dynamic Range:	better than 90 dB
• Wow and Flutter:	Unmeasurable
• Dimensions (W x H x D):	450 x 158 x 458 mm
• Fast Wind Time:	(17¹¹⁄₁₆″ x 6¼″ x 18¹⁄₁₆″)
• Error Correction:	70 sec (R120)
Dimensions (WxHxD):	(19″ x 6¼″ x 18¹⁄₁₆″)
• Weight (net):	44 lbs.

*Improvements may result in specification or feature changes with notice

© TEAC CORP. OF AMERICA, 7733 TELEGRAPH RD., MONTEBELLO, CA 90640   P.I. 3 88

122

Recorder Reproducer

☐ Two-speed, 1⅞ and 3¾ ips ☐ True 3-Head Record/Reproduce System ☐ Integral Dolby HX-Headroom Expansion System ☐ VU-type meters with Peak reading LED's ☐ Optional dbx interface ☐ Front panel Bias and EQ calibration

Specifications: 122

MECHANICAL

Tape: Standard compact cassette, C-60 and C-90 (Philips type)
Track Format: 4 track, 2 channel
Tape Speed: 1⅞ ips, 3¾ ips ±0.5%
Fast Wind Time: 90 seconds for C-60
Wow and Flutter:[1] 1⅞ ips ±0.18 % (IEC/ANSI/DIN weighted)
  ±0.08 % (IEC/ANSI/DIN unweighted)
  0.06 % (NAB weighted)
  0.11 % (NAB unweighted)
  [2]3¾ ips ±0.05 % (IEC/ANSI/DIN weighted)
  ±0.13 % (IEC/ANSI/DIN unweighted)
  0.04 % (NAB weighted)
  0.07 % (NAB unweighted)
Capstan Motor: DC servo motor
Reel Motor: DC motor
Head Configurations: 3-head, erase, record and reproduce

Dimensions: W 19" x H 5.8" x D 13.6" (482 x 147 x 345 mm)
Weighted: 19.8 pounds (9 kg)

ELECTRICAL

Line Input: (Line 1/Line 2)
  Input impedance: 50k ohms, unbalanced
  Maximum source impedance: 10k ohms or less
  Nominal input level: −24 dBV (63 mV)
  Minimum input level: −14 dBV (200 mV)
Line Output:
  Output impedance: 1.5k ohms, unbalanced
  Nominal load impedance: 10k ohms
  Nominal output level: −10 dBV (0.3 V)
  Maximum output level: −7.5 dBV (0.42 V)
Headphone Maximum Output: 100 mW at 8 ohms, stereo headphones
Equalization: 3¾ ips 3,180 μs + 35 μs METAL and high-bias tape,
  3,180 μs + 50 μs Normal-bias tape, switchable
  1⅞ ips 3,180 μs + 70 μs METAL and high-bias tape
  3,180 μs + 120 μs Normal-bias tape
Recording Level Calibration: 0 VU is referenced to 1 kHz, 160 nWb/m
  LED's present to turn "on" at a signal level of +8 VU
Total Harmonic Distortion:[2]
  0 VU, 160 nWb/m, 1 kHz
  3¾ ips 1% METAL
  1% Hi-bias
  1% Normal
  1⅞ ips 1.3% METAL
  1.2% Hi-bias
  1.5% Normal
  3% THD level
  3¾ ips 8 dB above 0 VU, 402 nWb/m METAL
  10 dB above 0 VU, 506 nWb/m Hi-bias
  8 dB above 0 VU, 402 nWb/m Normal
  1⅞ ips 7 dB above 0 VU, 358 nWb/m METAL
  9 dB above 0 VU, 451 nWb/m Hi-bias
  7 dB above 0 VU, 358 nWb/m Normal
Signal to Noise Ratio: At a reference of 1 kHz 3% THD level.

	A weighted	unweighted	A WTD with dbx	un-WTD with dbx	Tape
3¾ ips	60 dB	56 dB	91 dB	76 dB	METAL
	63 dB	58 dB	92 dB	77 dB	Hi-bias
	60 dB	55 dB	91 dB	76 dB	Normal
1⅞ ips	58 dB	53 dB	91 dB	73 dB	METAL
	58 dB	55 dB	92 dB	74 dB	Hi-bias
	56 dB	51 dB	91 dB	73 dB	Normal

When Dolby noise reduction is used for record and reproduce, the Signal to Noise Ratio will be improved by 5 dB at 1,000 Hz and by 10 dB at frequencies above 5,000 Hz.

Frequency Response:[2] Record/Reproduce

	METAL	Hi-base	Normal	Level
3¾ ips ±3 dB	35-14 kHz	35-14 kHz	35-14 kHz	0 VU
	35-24 kHz	35-20 kHz	35-18 kHz	−20 VU
1⅞ ips ±2 dB	35-14 kHz	35-8.3 kHz	35- 8 kHz	0 VU
	35-20 kHz	35-14 kHz	35-14 kHz	−20 VU

Adjacent Channel Separation: Better than 35 dB at 1 kHz
Erasure: Better than 65 dB at 1 kHz, +10 dB above 0 VU
Head Room: Recording amplifier: Better than 19 dB above 0 VU
  Reproduce amplifier: Better than 19 dB above 0 VU
Power Requirements: 117 V, 60 Hz, 25 watts

In these specifications, 0 dBV is referenced to 1.0 Volt
Actual voltage levels also are given in parenthesis. To calculate the 0 dB − 0.775 volt reference level (i.e. 0 dBm in a 600-ohm circuit) add 2.2 dB to the listed dB value; i.e., −10 dB re: 1 V − −7.8 dB re: 0.775 V.
(1) Specifications were determined using TEAC Test Tape MTT-111
(2) Metal specifications were determined using TEAC Test Tape MTT-507
  High Bias specifications were determined using TEAC Test Tape MTT-506
  Normal specifications were determined using TEAC Test Tape MTT-501
* dbx is a trademark of dbx, Inc.
Changes in specifications and features may be made without notice or obligation.

SPECIFICATIONS

MSR-24/16

MECHANICAL CHARACTERISTICS

Tape:
MSR 24 & 24S:	1 inch, 1.5 mil
MSR 16 & 16S:	1/2 inch, 1.5 mil

Track Format:
MSR 24 & 24S:	24-track, 24-channel
MSR 16 & 16S:	16-track, 16-channel

Head Configuration:	1 erase, 1 record/reproduce

Motor:
Capstan:	Phase locked loop DC direct drive motor x 1
Reel:	Slotless DC motor x 2
Reel size (max.):	10.5 inch, NAB hub
Tape Speed/Accuracy:	15 ips (38 cm/s) and 7.5 ips (19 cm/s)±0.2%
Pitch Control Range:	± 15% (both in Record and Reproduce)

Wow and Flutter:
15 ips:	± 0.06% peak (DIN weighted)
7.5 ips:	± 0.08% peak (DIN weighted)
Start Time:	0.5 sec. or less (10.5 inch reel, 2,400-ft tape)
Fast Wind Time:	120 sec. or less (10.5 inch reel, 2,400-ft tape)
Weight (net):	Main unit: 33 kg
	Power Supply unit: 15 kg

ELECTRICAL CHARACTERISTICS

Line Input:	-10 dBV/50 k ohms, unbalanced
Line Output:	10 dBV/220 ohms, unbalanced
Bias/Erase Frequency:	145 kHz

Equalization:
15 ips:	∞ +35 μsec. (IEC/CCIR)
7.5 ips:	∞ +70 μsec. (IEC/CCIR)
Operating Level:	250 nWb / m (0VU)

PERFORMANCE

Overall Frequency Response:
15 ips:	40 Hz to 20 kHz ± 3dB (at 0 VU)
7.5 ips:	40 Hz to 16 kHz ± 3 dB (at -10 VU)

Total Harmonic Distortion
(THD):	0.8% or less at 1,000 Hz, 0 VU
	(both at 15 and 7.5 ips)

Signal to-Noise Ratio
(ref. to 3% THD)

MSR 24
15 ips:	108 dB ("A" weighted, with dbx)
	65 dB ("A" weighted, without dbx)
7.5 ips:	105 dB ("A" weighted, with dbx)
	60 dB ("A" weighted, without dbx)

MSR 16
15 ips:	108 dB ("A" weighted, with dbx)
	65 dB ("A" weighted, without dbx)
7.5 ips:	105 dB ("A" weighted, with dbx)
	60 dB ("A" weighted, without dbx)

MSR 24S
15 ips:	93 dB (CCIR/ARM, with Dolby S)
	68 dB (CCIR/ARM, without Dolby S)
7.5 ips:	91 dB (CCIR/ARM, with Dolby S)
	65 dB (CCIR/ARM, without Dolby S)

MSR 16S
15 ips:	92 dB (CCIR/ARM, with Dolby S)
	68 dB (CCIR/ARM, without Dolby S)
7.5 ips:	90 dB (CCIR/ARM, with Dolby S)
	65 dB (CCIR/ARM, without Dolby S)

Crosstalk
(between Adjacent Channels):	80 dB or better (1,000 Hz, 0 VU, dbx IN)
	70 dB or better (1,000 Hz, 0 VU, with Dolby S)
Erasure:	70 dB or better (1,000 Hz, +10 VU)
Headroom (Record Amp):	28 dB or more (1,000 Hz, 0 VU)

- *In these specifications: 0 dBV is referenced to 1.0 volt.*
- *dbx is a registered trade mark of AKG Acoustics, Inc.*
- *Dolby the Double D symbol is a trademark of Dolby Laboratories Licensing Corporation.*
- *Changes in specifications and features may be made without notice or obligation.*

TSR-8

MECHANICAL CHARACTERISTICS

Tape:	1/2 inch (12.7 mm), 1.5 mil
Track Format:	8-track, 8-channel
Head Configuration:	1 erase, 1 record/reproduce

Motor:
Capstan:	FG servo DC motor
Reel:	DC motor x 2
Reel:	10.5-inch, NAB hub
Tape Speed:	15 ips (38 cm/s)
Pitch Control Range:	±12% (both in Record and Reproduce)
Wow and Flutter:	±0.06 peak (DIN weighted)
Start Time:	0.8 sec. or less
Fast Wind Time:	120 sec. or less (10.5-inch reel, 2400-ft tape)
Weight:	25 kg (55 1/4 lbs)

ELECTRICAL

Line Input (Unbalanced):	-10 dBV/10 kohms (ch. 1-7)
	-30 dBV~ +4 dBu/10 kohms (ch. 8)
Line Output (Unbalanced):	-10 dBV/100 ohms
Bias/Erase Frequency:	145 kHz
Equalization:	∞ +35 μsec. (IEC/CCIR)
Operating Level:	250 nWb/m (0 VU)
Power Consumption:	95 W

PERFORMANCE

Frequency Response
(rec/repro):	40 Hz to 20 kHz ± 3 dB (at 0 VU)
THD:	0.8 % or less at 1,000 Hz, 0 VU
Signal-To-Noise Ratio:	108 dB ("A" weighted, with DBX)
	68 dB ("A" weighted, without DBX)
Crosstalk:	82 dB or better (1,000 Hz, 0 VU, with DBX)
Erasure:	70 dB or better (1,000 Hz, +10 VU)

- *0 dBV=1V, 0 dBu=0.775V.*
- *dbx is a registered trademark of AKG Acoustics, Inc.*
- *Changes in specifications and features may be made without notice or obligation.*

MSR-24/24S

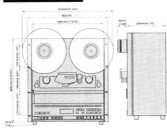

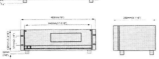

MSR-16/16S

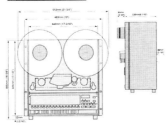

TSR-8

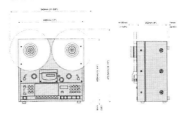

TEAC AMERICA, INC.
7733 Telegraph Road, Montebello, California 90640 Phone: (213) 726-0303

Printed in USA 0993E25M T1060029

TASCAM®

Take advantage of our experience.

DA-88 Technical Specifications

Transport	
Recording System:	Rotary, 4 head Digital recording 8mm, Hi-8 cassette
Recording Time:	100 minutes approx per Hi-8 cassette
Fast Forward/Rewind Rate:	80 seconds (x100)
Audio Scan Rate:	x¼ ~ x9
Audio	
Number of Tracks:	Eight
Audio Conversion: Record (A/D) Conversion:	16 bit linear, one bit Delta Sigma x 64 Delta Sigma
Play (D/A) Conversion:	18 bit linear, single converter per channel x 8fs
Sample Rate:	44.1 & 48kHz
Variable Pitch:	±6% & ±6%
Frequency Response:	20Hz ~ 20kHz ± 0.5dB
Dynamic Range:	Greater than 93dB
Distortion:	Less than 0.007% THD
Channel Crosstalk:	Better than −90dB 1kHz
Wow & Flutter:	Unmeasurable
Digital I/O:	D-sub 25 pin
Analog I/O:	−10dB RCA pin +4 Bal, D-sub 25 pin
Meter Out:	D-sub 15 pin w/DC
System Lockup Connectors:	D-sub 15 pin
System Lockup Capabilities:	Automatic lock between DA-88's up to 16 DA-88's (128 audio tracks)
Word Sync In/Out:	Std speed clock Digital domain
General Information	
Power Consumption:	90 watt
Dimensions (W x H x D):	19.0" x 6.89" x 14.6" (4U)
Weight:	33 lbs
Optional Accessories	
RC-848	System Remote Controller
RC-808	Single Remote Controller
SY-88	Synchronization Board
IF-88AE	AES/EBU Interface
IF-88SD	S/DIF-2 Interface

© 1992 TEAC America, Inc.
Preliminary information only.
Specifications and features subject to change without notice.

MAIN FEATURES

- Hi-8mm cassette tape which allows approximately 100 minutes of recording time on a standard 120 tape. Audio for feature length films and entire CDs can be recorded on one tape.

- Tascam rugged and proven professional transport.

- Large transport buttons for Fast Forward, Rewind, Stop, Play and Record functions under 15-segment LED meters.

- Large Jog/Shuttle wheel for easy locating on tape.

- No formatting of tape before recording.

- Single button record Punch-In.

- Rehearsal mode allows user to rehearse without recording on tape.

- 8-digit LED time display shows absolute time in Hours, Minutes, Seconds and Frames as well as displaying Memo times, pitch change, SMPTE Time Code and SMPTE Offset.

- Optional SY-88 Synchronization Board (attaches with two sets of screws to a rear panel of the DA-88) provides SMPTE synchronization, both as master and slave, video sync, a 9-pin RS-422 port, and MMC (MIDI Machine Control).

TASCAM®

Early Price Sheets

TASCAM CORPORATION

5440 McConnell Avenue • Los Angeles, Calif. 90066

(213) 390-3566

TEAC CALIBRATION AND ALIGNMENT TAPE

Price List Effective August 1, 1973

CASSETTE

Item No.	Name	Frequencies	Level	Tolerances	User's Net
MTT-111	Speed Deviation Check For instantaneous and long term speed deviation analysis	3kHz	-10dB	.07% WTD (Rms) Maximum Inherent Flutter	$20.00
MTT-112	Standard Operating Level	333Hz	0dB	250 nWb/m	
MTT-113	Azimuth Standard	6.3kHz	-10dB	$90^o \pm 2$ min	18.00
MTT-114	Azimuth Standard	10kHz	-10dB	$90^o \pm 2$ min	
MTT-115	Frequency Alignment Reference	333Hz, 6kHz	-10dB	± 1dB Maximum Deviation	21.00
MTT-116L	Frequency Alignment Reference	40-10kHz	0 & -10dB	± 1dB Maximum Deviation	48.00
MTT-117	Frequency Alignment Reference	125Hz, 1kHz, 6.3kHz	-10dB	± 1dB Maximum Deviation	
MTT-118	Standard Reference Level	1kHz	-10dB	± 0.5dB Maximum Deviation	
MTT-121	Crosstalk Check For Half Track	1kHz	-10dB	60dB Maximum Inherent Crosstalk	23.00
MTT-141	Crosstalk Check For Quarter Track	1kHz	-10dB	55dB Maximum Inherent Crosstalk	
MTT-150	Standard B Dolby Level Produced to meet the specifications of Dolby Labs Inc. Dolby is a reg. Td. Mk. of Dolby Labs Inc.	400Hz, 420Hz	0dB	200 nWb/m	18.00

OPEN REEL

Item No.	Name	Speed	Frequencies	Level	Tolerances	User's Net
YTT-1002	Frequency Alignment	3 3/4 ips	50Hz-10kHz	0	± 0.5dB Maximum Deviation	
YTT-1003	Reference	7 1/2 ips	40Hz-15kHz	and		$25.00
YTT-1004		15 ips	30Hz-20kHz	-10dB		
YTT-2002	Speed Deviation Check	3 3/4 ips			0.07% WTD Rms*	
YTT-2003	for instantaneous and	7 1/2 ips	3kHz	-5dB	0.05% WTD Rms*	
YTT-2004	long term speed variation analysis	15 ips			0.03% WTD Rms*	

*Maximum Inherent Flutter

All prices (subject to change without notice) are FOB Los Angeles and include shielded metal cannister.

These precision tapes are produced by the Standards Laboratory of TEAC Audio Systems Corporation, Japan. Distributed by TASCAM Corporation.

Though located in Marina Del Rey, the McConnell Avenue office on this August 1, 1973, price list was listed as a Los Angeles address before the new Marina neighborhood received its own zip code.

TASCAM CORPORATION
5440 McCONNELL AVENUE · LOS ANGELES, CALIF. 90066

ALL PRICES INDICATED ARE FAIR TRADED

January, 1974

	U.S.A. USER's NET
MODEL 10 MIXING CONSOLES	
8-in, 4-out	$1890.00
12-in, 4-out	2490.00
16-in, 4-out) Model 10 + Model 100	3375.00
24-in, 4-out)	4575.00

For nominal 200 Ohm mic inputs, add $15.50 per channel (Model 109 & 210). For nominal 600 Ohm or bridging line inputs, add $15.50 per channel (Model 110 and 210 or 211 -- there are line inputs on the 102 Submasters to provide for simultaneous buss tape monitoring). For nominal + 4 dBm line outputs, add $200.00 for two channels. $400.00 for four channels (Model 113).

ACCESSORIES

Model 100 Expander (with expander module and connector cable)	285.00
Model 101 Input Module	150.00
Model 104-A Talkback Module with Slate (includes mic and 5W amplifier)	210.00
Model 105 Remote Control Module with 15 foot connector cable (factory wired for TASCAM control circuits)	90.00
Model 106 Monitor Mixdown Module (with pan)	210.00
Model 107 Quad Panner Module (4 joy sticks)	210.00
Model 108 Headphone Monitor Panel (with independent channel assignments for each ear can)	120.00
Model 109 Mic Input Transformer (single channel, nominal 200 Ohms)	14.50
Model 110 Line Input Transformer (single channel, specify 600 Ohms or bridging)	14.50
Model 111 Double Size Filler Panel	10.00
Model 112 Single Size Filler Panel	9.00

> NOTE: All initial orders are filled with the necessary filler panels. When accessories are ordered at a later date, buyer must determine the number and size of filler panels required.

Model 113 Line Amplifier (two channels with built-in power supply)	200.00
Model 117 Pedestal Base for Model 10	150.00
Model 118 Pedestal Base for Model 100	150.00
Model 210 Transformer Bracket (for Model 101 Input Module)	1.00
Model 211 Transformer Bracket (for Model 102 Submaster Module)	1.00
Model 217 Set of 4 Legs with mounting hardware (for Model 10 or Model 100)	12.00

TASCAM Corporation price list for January 1974; a few months before the company was purchased by TEAC.

TEAC PROFESSIONAL PRODUCTS

7733 Telegraph Road
Montebello, California 90640
(213) 726-0303

Price Schedule C1
SEPTEMBER 15, 1974

MINIMUM
FAIR TRADE
RESALE *

Products

Model 10 Mixing Consoles

8-in, 4-out, High Z	$2350.00
12-in, 4-out, High Z	3110.00
16-in, 4-out, High Z	4245.00
24-in, 4-out, High Z	5765.00

Series 70 Recorder/Reproducers

(Quarter-inch Configurations)

Two Channel 701 Electronics	$1700.00
Two Channel 501 Electronics	2000.00
Four Channel 701 Electronics	1950.00

(Half-inch Configurations)

Four Track 701 Electronics	2750.00
Four Track 501 Electronics	3100.00
Eight Track 701 Electronics	4600.00

All recorders are shipped ready for rack mount and are biased for 3M no.206 tape unless otherwise specified at the time of order.

Some quarter-inch configurations other than those listed are available upon request.

Parts

Model 100	Expander	$ 375.00
Model 101	Input Module	190.00
Model 102	Submaster Module	115.00
Model 103	Master Gain Module	60.00
Model 104A	Talkback Module with Slate	260.00
Model 105	Remote Control Module	130.00
Model 106	Monitor Mixdown Module	265.00
Model 107	Quad Panner Module	265.00
Model 108	Headphone Monitor Panel	150.00
Model 109	Mic Input Transformer (Not installed)	17.00
Model 110	Line Input Transformer (Not installed)	17.00
Model 111	Double Size Filler Panel	12.50
Model 112	Single Size Filler Panel	12.50
Model 113	Line Amplifier	250.00
Model 117	Pedestal Base for Model 10	190.00
Model 118	Pedestal Base for Model 110	190.00
Model 210	Transformer Bracket (For Model 101-not installed)	1.00
Model 211	Transformer Bracket (For Model 102-not installed)	1.00
Model 217	Set of 4 Legs with Mounting Hardware (For Model 10 or Model 100)	12.00

Terms: 5% 30 days *APPLIES IN STATES WHERE FAIR TRADE LAWS ARE APPLICABLE.   **F.O.B. Los Angeles**

Dealer price list from September 15, 1974; just after the TEAC acquisition and move to Montebello.

Author's Note

Randy Alberts is a California-based author, musician, and audio engineer who has published over 300 articles for pro and consumer music, audio, recording, computer, and new media magazines and websites since 1983. Born in Denver, Colorado, and raised on the Beatles, baseball, and So Cal's beaches, his career in publishing moved from printing *Newsweek* and *Sunset* at R.R. Donnelley to music journalism with *Radio & Records*, *Mix*, and *Electronic Musician* magazines before moving north to the S.F. Bay in 1989. He joined the original *EQ* and *Keyboard* in advertising sales roles before becoming a freelance writer in 1995. Alberts contributed a chapter to *Interactivity in Action* (Miller Freeman Books) in 1997 about an experimental Japanese multimedia company and authored a story for *Computer Life* magazine that same year showing home PC users how to make music and jam with easy-to-use music creation software; the latter won the Computer Press Awards' Best Individual How-To Article of The Year honor for Ziff-Davis Publishing and the author.

Currently interviewing high profile artists, producers, songwriters, sound designers, and engineers for Digidesign's website and authoring how-to application stories, reviews, and product guides for *Mix*, *Remix*, *Electronic Musician* and other leading audio and music publications, Alberts is also an Editorial Associate with the Montara Creative Group in San Francisco and has been AV Video Multimedia Producer's Contributing Audio Editor since 1996.

His personal music credits include a new electro-acoustic CD called *Begin Again and More Than Words*, a collection of alternate-tuned guitar compositions from 1996; original music and sound design for *Mix*'s 1988 TEC Awards Show in Los Angeles with George Martin, Quincy Jones, and Les Paul sitting at the first table; a number of small-market radio spots over the years; eight years on guitar for Presentense, a well-amplified '80s rock/pop group from West L.A., at places like Madame Wongs, The Troubadour, and All The Way Live; and currently recording, mixing, and burning discs for local Bay area musicians, producers, and organizations, including LittleKidsRock.org.

Alberts still refers to his first Portastudio as the most important musical instrument he's ever played; 25 years later he's converting yet another dwelling into a studio, this time OpenDoor Edit/Audio, an editorial desk, audio service, and music creation studio with a view (www.opendooredit.com, au-dio@pacbell.net.)

Index